A Hund
Merry 7

CW00816030

John Rastell

A Hundred Merry Tales

THE SHAKESPEARE JEST BOOK

edited by
John Thor Ewing

WELKIN BOOKS

First published in hardback 2018
Paperback edition 2018
Welkin Books Ltd

ISBN 978-1-910075-08-1

Acknowledgements

It's now twenty years since, whilst browsing the shelves of the Public Library in Newcastle-upon-Tyne, I first encountered *A Hundred Merry Tales*. At some time or another since then, I've probably shared these stories with just about everyone I know, and I have also used them in storytelling performances. In particular, I should mention Brian Holton, Steve Whitt, Sean Breadin and my brother Peter Ewing, for their willingness to humour my interest in these tales, and for allowing me to formulate my ideas about what I believe to be their real importance in the story of English literature.

Special mention is due for Nia Powell of Bangor University who has been good enough to help me correct the section of the introduction relating to Wales, to Harriet Tarlo for checking through the section on misogyny in the tales, and to Cathy Shrank of Sheffield University and Paul Halsall for helping locate the reference in *Civil and Uncivil Life*. Thanks are also due to Madeleine Cox and the Reader Services Team at the Shakespeare Birthplace Trust, Nicola Hudson and the staff of the Rare Books Department and Manuscript Reading Room at Cambridge University Library, and to the staff of the Rare Books and Music Reading Room at the British Library.

I should also note that all price comparisons are based on information from the National Archives website, comparing prices in 1520 with their approximate equivalent spending power in 2017. Rastell's woodcuts are reproduced either from the facsimile of the second edition of *A Hundred Merry Tales*, or from *The Pastyme of People* as digitised and kindly made available by Boston Public Library.

My wife Annie has been especially helpful, discussing many of the tales with me, and her insights have been both useful and interesting.

But mine, all mine, is responsibility for the errors!

JTE

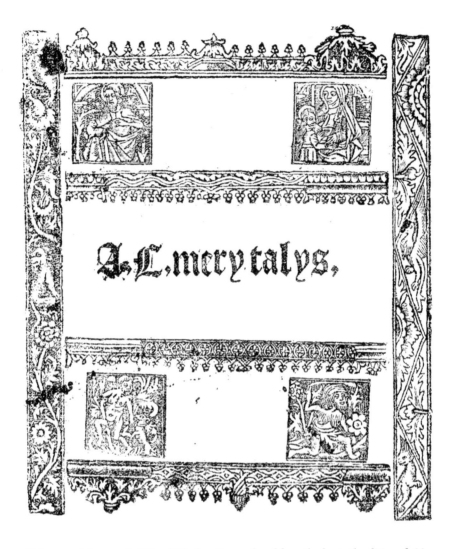

Title page of the second edition ('B') of 1526, reproduced from the facsimile edition of 1887.

Contents

Introduction

After its publication some 500 years ago, *A Hundred Merry Tales* came to be acknowledged as one of the classics of English letters. It was followed by a succession of imitators such as *Merry Tales and Quick Answers* (c.1532-5) and *The Jests of Scoggin* (c.1565-6), but sixteenth-century readers continued to hold this first English jest book in especially high regard. Celebrated by such great writers as Shakespeare and Dekker, it would be to this book that the dying Elizabeth I would turn for solace and amusement in the closing days of Tudor England, and it was one of the very first English books to be at least partially republished north of the border after the accession of the Scottish king James Stuart to the throne of England in 1603.

Like much of the literature of Tudor England, *A Hundred Merry Tales* slipped almost into oblivion during the seventeenth century, but whereas many other works were revived after the Restoration, *A Hundred Merry Tales* was given up for lost, and when, in the nineteenth century, copies of two separate editions were at last discovered, the humour of the tales was judged too crude for prudish Victorian tastes, and it failed to regain its former acclaim.

The first English jest book

A Hundred Merry Tales is rightly acclaimed as the earliest English jest book, but what exactly is a jest book? Although the jest books of sixteenth and seventeenth century England were the forerunners of the joke books of today, a Tudor jest is not the same as a modern joke. While these jests are intended to be merry, many also have a moral or mnemonic aspect which is often at least as important as the comedy. So, it is better to approach *A Hundred Merry Tales* as a book of droll or amusing anecdotes rather than as a book of jokes.

Like a Tudor jest, a modern anecdote does not necessarily have to be hilariously funny, but may be thought-provoking in any number of ways. Humour, like learning, was not an end in itself for the medieval or Renaissance thinker; it was a path which could be directed either towards virtue or vice. So, a worthy book of merry tales should include tales which were not only funny, but which would direct its readers on the path of virtue.

When this book was rediscovered in Victorian times, commentators were not only disturbed by what they perceived as the 'coarseness' of Tudor humour, they were simultaneously perplexed by what they considered its 'insipid' quality. This may be partly deliberate. While the Tudor humorist has no qualms about discussing sex and bodily functions, using words which were absolutely taboo to his Victorian descendants, he seems oddly wary of provoking laughter in his reader. Even in the funniest tales, the storyteller seems sometimes to avoid unleashing the full force of his comedy, preferring to approach comic scenarios obliquely, so that the reader is able to appreciate the joke rather than to experience its humour directly. The aim is to raise a knowing smile rather than a belly laugh. To guffaw openly could reveal a loss of control, which for a sixteenth-century reader might be considered indecorous or unseemly. So, although several tales describe laughter, we as readers are invited to observe the joke rather than to indulge in the full absurdity of the situation.

Jest books elsewhere

Like so much else that typifies the English Renaissance, the Tudor jest book has Continental forerunners, most significantly the Latin *Facetiae* of the scholar and Papal Secretary Poggio Bracciolini (1380-1459) which were published in 1470. In an afterword, Poggio says his tales were drawn from tall stories and gossip which had circulated in the Vatican earlier in his career, and he named individual raconteurs whose contribution had been particularly significant. Thus, the stories themselves are part of a tradition of medieval humour, but Poggio's *Facetiae* differed from earlier collections of amusing tales, such as Bocaccio's *Decameron*, in that his stories were brief anecdotes, succinctly told and without any attempt to construct a narrative frame. Poggio's innovation was to liberate jests or *facetiae* from the encumbrance of formal literary structure and pretension.

Other Continental collections of *facetiae* appeared in the fifty years which separate Poggio's *Facetiae* and *A Hundred Merry Tales*. Most were in Latin and were liberally sprinkled with retellings of stories from Classical tradition. One such collection of Latin *facetiae* was the *Convivium fabulosum* of Erasmus, published in 1524—Erasmus was a leading light of the humanist circle which included Rastell, publisher and probable author of the *Merry Tales*, and his Latin jest book must have been completed at around the same time as the *Merry Tales*, which were published in 1524-5.

But this first English jest book is no simple imitation of foreign exemplars. *A Hundred Merry Tales* is strikingly different from earlier collections of *facetiae*, with a distinctive character of its own which is recognisably English in style. Most obviously, it is written not in Latin but in the English vernacular, many of the tales are set in London or in the surrounding countryside, most do not seem to have any written sources, and, whether set in town or country, the settings are invariably English in character.

Textual Criticism

Before proceeding to the life of author and publisher John Rastell (p.30) and considering the *Tales* in their sixteenth-century context (p.36), it is necessary first to analyse the surviving sources, how they relate to one another, and what this can tell us about the early publication history and authorship of *A Hundred Merry Tales*.

Surviving original copies

A Hundred Merry Tales survives principally in two black-letter folio editions, both printed in the sixteenth century by the press of John Rastell, one of which is dated to 22 November 1526. A few pages from another English edition of c.1548 are also extant, and forty seven of the tales were printed in 1603 by Robert Charteris in Edinburgh.

A Hundred Merry Tales was first rediscovered for modern readers in 1815 by the scholar John Josias Conybeare, who found pages from two or more copies of the same edition, which had been re-used as pasteboard in the binding of a more-or-less contemporary volume. Many of the leaves have been badly damaged, but by a comparison of all the surviving parts, a substantial portion of this book has been retrieved. Nevertheless, aside from various minor *lacunae*, there are twenty six tales where several lines are missing, and a further six tales are very badly damaged. The text was edited and published by Samuel Weller Singer in 1815, and Singer's transcription was reprinted with notes by William Carew Hazlitt in 1864—Hazlitt believed that this edition had been printed in about 1525 (Hazlitt 1864, p.3) and, more recently, Devereux has dated it to 1524-5 (Devereux 1999, p.113). Conybeare's discovery now survives as two fragmentary copies, one of which is preserved in the British Library, and the other is held by the Shakespeare Birthplace Trust in Stratford-Upon-Avon. I have chosen to refer to Conybeare's edition (STC 23663, Devereux No.15) as 'A', and to number its selection of tales from A.1 to A.100. The numbering in the original unaccountably skips from 97 directly to 99, so there is no tale A.98, and this edition thus includes a total of just ninety nine merry tales.

A unique copy of another edition from Rastell's press was discovered in 1864 by Dr Hermann Oesterley in the library of the University of Göttingen (*Niedersächsische Staats und Universitätsbibliothek*, Göttingen), which had been purchased in 1767 in Lüneburg. This copy is complete and well preserved, consisting of 28 leaves in folio, and it is dated 22 November 1526 at the Sign of the Mermaid at Paul's Gate next to Cheapside. Its text was published in a critical edition by Oesterley in 1866, and in a facsimile edition by Hazlitt in 1887. This edition (STC 23664, Devereux No.35) is referred to henceforth as 'B' and its tales are numbered B.1 to B.100.

Although Rastell's two editions are substantially the same and are printed by the same press, there are also significant differences between them, most importantly that Tales 2, 7, 91 and 98 were never included in 'A', while Tales 101, 102 and 103 are similarly absent from 'B'.

Four leaves survive from an octavo edition, probably printed c.1548 by Robert Copland. They have been reused as flyleaves for a copy of Bishop Stephen Gardiner's *An Explication and Assertion of the true Catholique Fayth* (1551) which bears the autograph of the merchant Edward Castelyn, and is now kept in Cambridge University Library. This edition (STC 23664.5) will be referred to as 'C' with tales numbered C.1 to C.12. Two of the tales which survive in 'C' (101 & 102) are among those printed in 'A' but omitted from 'B', while Tale 100, which is known from both 'A' and 'B', appears never to have formed part of this edition.

Forty seven of the *Merry Tales* were reprinted by Robert Charteris in Edinburgh in 1603 to accompany a quarto edition of a poem in early Scots called *The Three Tales of the Three Priests of Peebles*, where they are described as 'sundry merry tales very pleasant to the reader, and more exactly corrected than the former impression.' This edition (STC 19528) survives in three copies, now in the National Library of Scotland, the Bodleian Library and the Folger Shakespeare Library. It is referred to here as 'D', and its tales numbered from D.1 to D.47. The titles of the tales in 'D' tend to reflect titles used in 'B' rather than 'A', but whereas 'D' does not reprint any of the four tales in 'B' which are not found in 'A', it does print all three of the tales from 'A' which are omitted from 'B'—like 'C', it too omits Tale 100.

The four editions, 'A', 'B', 'C' & 'D'

The relationship between the two surviving Rastell editions of *A Hundred Merry Tales* has been the subject of some speculation. Oesterley (1866, p.viii-xiii) argued emphatically that 'B' was the original edition, and that 'A' was copied from the printed text of 'B' incorporating certain deliberate changes and corrections as well as introducing new mistakes. Writing in 1887, Hazlitt expressed serious reservations about this opinion, but it was not until 1999 that Edward James Devereux over-turned Oesterley's arguments by pointing out that a large decorative printing block had clearly been damaged before it was used in the printing of 'B' while the same block was undamaged when used to print 'A'. Devereux believed the damage to this printing block occurred in 1525, and dated the printing of 'A' to c.1524-5. According to Devereux, 'A' is 'the last [of Rastell's books] to contain the large device without border damage. It also marks the first appearance of the 220 textura.'

It is however unlikely that 'B' is directly copied from 'A'. The fact that the numbers ascribed to individual tales vary between 'A' and 'B' while the general sequence of tales is preserved, suggests instead that both editions may have drawn on a common source in which the tales were written in order but without numbers—the radically different position of Tale 43 (A.33/B.43) in the two editions could suggest that this shared source included some loose leaves among its pages, although this tale may have been deliberately moved for editorial reasons. The common copy text must have included more than one hundred tales, allowing 'A' and 'B' to offer differing selections, so that there is a total of a hundred and three tales across the two editions. This interpretation would appear to be confirmed by the fact that most of the errors in each edition are unique to that version of the text, whereas, if 'B' had been based on 'A' or *vice versa*, we should expect many of the errors to be repeated—one apparent example of such a repeated error in the extant copies does occur in Tale 37 (A.36/B.37), which may be due to error or confusion in the copy text.

Sixteenth-century orthography may always appear somewhat arbitrary by modern standards, but the differing approaches of 'A' and 'B' to English spelling are plain enough that even the untrained reader can tell that the text of these two editions has been prepared by two different hands. While 'A' appears either to have been type-set by Rastell himself or by his printer Thomas Kele, the type-setter of 'B' has been identified as Peter Treveris, a jobbing printer who was working in Southwark between 1522 and 1532, often as a sub-contractor for established printers, including Rastell.

Robert Copland's edition of c.1548, 'C', included some if not all of the tales which appeared in 'A' but which had been omitted from 'B', and when Robert Charteris came to select tales for his edition, 'D', in 1603, he also included all those tales which appear in 'A' rather than 'B' and none which are unique to 'B'; both later editions, 'C' and 'D', also omit Tale 100. Thus, Tales 101-3 do not appear in 'B' but are reprinted in 'D' (101 and 102 also survive in the fragmentary 'C'), whereas Tales 2, 7, 91 and 98 do not appear 'A' and are also absent from both 'C' and 'D'. However, the titles in 'D' for Tales 4, 5, 8 and 44 are apparently derived from titles as given in 'B', and differ from the titles for the same tales in 'A', which suggests that Charteris must have based his text on a sixteenth-century reprint which reconciled differences between Rastell's two original editions 'A' and 'B'; this could have been either Copland's edition of c.1548, 'C', or a similar lost edition.

Although the copyright for printing *A Hundred Merry Tales* passed through several hands during the sixteenth century, the revision of the text is more likely to have been done by Rastell himself, and to have been printed by his press before his death in 1536. It is not hard to understand why Rastell might have felt such a revision necessary. Two of the new tales included by Treveris, Tale 91 'Of the maltman of Colnbrook,' and Tale 98 'Of a certain alderman's deeds of London,' are markedly unlike other tales in the collection, introducing a bitter tone which is at odds with the merriment suggested by the title.

In summary, 'A' is the earliest known edition, but the two extant copies survive only in fragmentary form and it never included the full quota of a hundred tales; 'B' is the only complete copy of a sixteenth-century edition, but comprises a slightly idiosyncratic selection of tales, which was rejected in subsequent editions; 'C' may represent a reprint of Rastell's final text, which resolved difficulties with both 'A' and 'B', and although it survives only in an extremely fragmentary form, helps reveal the shape of later editions; 'D' presents only a sample of the tales adapted for a Scottish readership but, by good fortune includes all the tales which are absent from 'B', allowing us to fill the remaining *lacunae* in the fragmentary text preserved in 'A', while its use of titles similar to 'B' reveals that the standard version of the text cannot have been identical with either 'A' or 'B'.

From a comparison of all four surviving editions, it is possible to suggest the following, partly-conjectural publication history of *A Hundred Merry Tales*:

'A' was almost certainly the first edition, and was prepared either by Rastell himself or by Thomas Kele from a manuscript commonplace book of more than a hundred tales collected from both oral and written sources. This edition was hastily withdrawn from sale when it was found to contain only ninety nine tales rather than the hundred promised in the title—as a lawyer and legal educator, Rastell may have been especially sensitive to the fault of issuing a book under a demonstrably misleading title. Some or all of the remaining unsold copies were then re-used as pasteboard for bindings of other books, which is how pages from more than one copy of this edition came to be discovered together.

If the title was withdrawn from sale despite continuing demand, Rastell would have been keen to have a new edition available as soon as possible and, perhaps because it was required at short notice, he delegated the type setting to Peter Treveris. This edition, 'B', comprised a full one hundred tales drawn from the same manuscript as 'A', and went to print on 22 November 1526. Rather than simply adding a single tale however, Treveris had made his own selection of tales from Rastell's manuscript and included some which may have been deliberately rejected by Rastell for inclusion among his *Merry Tales*. Although the choice of tales is different in 'B', the style of the additional tales is completely consistent with the authorial style of tales in 'A' and they are undoubtedly copied from the same source.

A lost third edition, probably also by Rastell, restored tales A.97-100 which Treveris had omitted from his edition, 'B', but used titles based on the Treveris edition; it probably also included tales B.2 and B.7, but omitted Tale 100 (A.96, B.100) along with B.91 and B.98.

After Rastell's death, a new edition 'C' was printed by Copland c.1548. The title was later entered to John Walley in 1557-8 (Arber I.75), and to John Charlwood on 15 January 1582 as the former property of Sampson Awdeley (John Sampson, d.1575; Arber II.405), and finally to James Roberts on 28-31 May 1594 (Arber II.651). Although in 1603 the license to print *A Hundred Merry Tales* was thus held by the London printer James Roberts, Robert Charteris in Edinburgh was able to print his own version because, despite the Union of the Crowns, he was was not subject to English law. Nevertheless, he may have been careful not to draw too much attention to his action, printing only a selection of the *Tales* as a marginal text in his edition of the *Three Priests of Peebles*.

This edition

In preparing the present edition, I have consulted all four extant source editions. Surviving fragments from the first edition 'A' were consulted at the British Library and Shakespeare Birthplace Trust, and the remaining pages of 'C' were consulted at Cambridge University Library, while editions 'B' and 'D' were consulted in facsimile.

I first encountered *A Hundred Merry Tales* through the text of 'A' as transcribed by Singer in 1815 and reprinted by Hazlitt in 1864. In his edition of 1866, Hermann Oesterley was cautious of this transcription, citing it as 'Hazlitt' rather than as an alternative Rastell edition. Although Singer's transcription is generally accurate, there are occasional misreadings, and some conjectural reconstructions have become confused with genuine readings from the original text. Singer also deliberately omitted any tales where too little text survived to allow a satisfying reconstruction, but even the sparsest of remains can shed valuable light on text preserved in other editions. These factors made it essential to return to the surviving original copies of what is almost certainly the first edition of *A Hundred Merry Tales*.

Oesterley's edition includes lengthy quotations from whatever sources he was able to identify for the tales, and he also traces the later publication history of some individual tales as late as the eighteenth or even nineteenth centuries—since Oesterley's edition is readily available in reprints and online editions, it has not seemed necessary to duplicate this work here; I have however included an increased number of early retellings, and have quoted these in full in the accompanying notes for each tale.

There is general agreement between all the sources throughout most of the text, but there are also notable variations, both accidental and deliberate, and wherever the original editions disagree, it has been necessary to choose a reading taken from one or more source texts over an alternative reading. Readings from each of the two editions from Rastell's own press, 'A' and 'B', have an obvious claim to priority, but because Rastell probably produced at least one more edition, now lost, on which later reprints were based, variant readings in 'C' and 'D' may actually represent deliberate emendations by Rastell.

As a result, wherever there is uncertainty over the best reading, a certain element of subjectivity has been inevitable. In almost all cases however, other factors have been sufficient to decide the question: thus, it is generally more likely that a word or phrase will have been omitted (either by accident or to save space on the page) than that extra text might have accidentally been added; and elsewhere, when two or more editions agree on one particular reading, this will usually be preferred to a single instance of an alternative reading. Textual variants are included in an Appendix on p.326.

Rather than comparing all four early editions, previous editors of the last two centuries have always drawn exclusively on either one of the two extant versions from Rastell's press, 'A' or more commonly 'B', and because the only complete early copy, 'B', includes a somewhat idiosyncratic choice of tales, this approach has been a significant hurdle to a proper appreciation of the original work. Because this new edition is unique in drawing on readings from all four source editions, it is the first ever edition to include all 103 of the tales, and it is also the first to restore rediscovered 'lost' passages from the original edition. This is thus the only edition which presents either a full or a corrected text of *A Hundred Merry Tales*.

Authorship

In the nineteenth century, it was thought possible that *A Hundred Merry Tales* was the work of Rastell's famous kinsman, Sir Thomas More. William Carew Hazlitt in particular considered the question of whether the *Hundred Merry Tales* were written by either Rastell's brother-in-law, Sir Thomas More, or his son-in-law, John Heywood. To Hazlitt, it seemed 'not at all improbable that the ... collection was made by John Heywood with the assistance, possibly at the instigation, of Sir Thomas More ...' (Hazlitt 1887, p.vii).

The rambling legalistic style of the tales is however so unlike More's elegant and polished English that an attribution of authorship to More seems thoroughly implausible. The suggestion that it is the work of Rastell's son-in-law John Heywood is only slightly more persuasive. Heywood was probably originally from Coventry, so the author's familiarity with Coventry priests (Tale 56) and with hunting at Stony Stratford (Tale 31) would be consistent with this attribution. But Heywood's personal connections were at the royal court and in the world of music, and neither of these *milieux* features significantly in the *Merry Tales*. Furthermore, Heywood represents a younger generation, whereas the *Tales* have the avuncular air of an old man's reminiscences.

Even Hazlitt concedes that the style of the *Tales* is sufficiently unlike either More or Heywood 'that there was a third hand in the affair—probably that of the printer and editor', and that More and Heywood were probably no more than 'contributors to its contents' (Hazlitt 1887, p.x). If the supposed role of More and Heywood amounted merely to the contribution of tales to the collection, then it is difficult to consider them as anything more than friends of the true author, who must be the 'printer and editor' John Rastell himself, whose characteristic style pervades the entire collection.

Devereux tentatively acknowledges Rastell as a possible author, writing, 'There is really no evidence that Rastell was himself the compiler, though the ponderous wit and diffuse prose do at least allow the possibility. Certainly, he was writing a lot in the 1520s and shifting his attention away from legal education towards humanist elegance and moral teaching' (Devereux 1999, p.114), which is as much as to say, there is no particular reason *not* to think that the *Tales* are the work of John Rastell, but the case has yet to be made.

Although the stories of the *Merry Tales* do not reflect any individual personal viewpoint, they do contain some pointers suggesting their authorship by Rastell. We have already alluded to the author's possible connection with Coventry. Rastell himself was born in Coventry where he was a member of the Corpus Christi Guild. He lived in Coventry until the age of thirty three, and succeeded his father as Coroner there in 1506. We might also detect a local connection for Tale 70 which is set in Barnet, where Rastell had a house at Monken Hadley from 1515.

Two of the tales show a particular interest in drama, whether in the Coventry Corpus Christi pageants of Tale 56, or in the Suffolk stage play of Tale 4 (which should probably be envisaged as a touring production with local amateur actors taking minor roles). It is also possible that local knowledge of the area around Stratford-upon-Avon in Tales 73 and 56 comes through touring stage plays, which were probably established there long before the young William Shakespeare's day—both Stratford and Shottery are, in any case, within twenty miles of Rastell's home town of Coventry. Rastell was closely connected with the early Tudor theatre. In 1522 he was chosen to write and direct the pageant performed in London at the king's meeting with Emperor Charles V, and five years later he did the same for the opening entertainment, on 5 May 1527, at the theatre at Greenwich which he had helped to decorate. Rastell not only wrote, directed, and possibly acted in his own plays, he was also the first printer to publish scripts, and in 1527-8 he established the first permanent dedicated theatre in England at Finsbury Fields. Rastell's own drama of the *Four Elements* (c.1519) is echoed in two of the tales, most obviously in Tale 19, 'Of the Four Elements, where they should soon be found', but also in Tale 9 which reworks a joke Rastell had used in his earlier play.

There is a noticeable fondness for lawyers and legal settings in the *Tales*, which suggests an author closely connected with the legal profession. Aside from several tales with a tangential interest in the law or in quasi-legal issues, lawyers of one sort or another are directly represented in seven tales (20, 26, 37, 48, 59, 63 and 94) and what is especially remarkable is the unexpectedly positive attitude which the author takes towards them, which contrasts markedly with the more critical attitude adopted towards the clergy. In Tale 37 we read of 'a good old gentleman being a lawyer' as if the two are more-or-less synonymous, and we even warm to the lawyer who is described in Tale 59 as a 'crafty man of law' although the joke is surely that most people would distrust lawyers because of their perceived craftiness and guile. Other tales reflect the concerns and interests of the legal profession: Tale 94 is a humorous example of lawyers' exasperation at the ignorance of unlearned jurors; while Tale 26, 'Of the gentleman that bore the segboard on his neck', has the flavour of a student tale passed down from one intake to the next among the young lawyers of Thavie's Inn, and perhaps Rastell first encountered it in his own days as an Utter Barrister at Middle Temple in 1502. Tales 48 and 98 are concerned with miscarriages of justice. Thus, on the basis of internal evidence, we might suggest that the author was a lawyer with an interest in the theatre who may originally have hailed from Coventry.

Another perspective on the authorship of the Tales is opened up through our understanding of the relationship between the surviving editions. When Treveris prepared the second edition, 'B', in 1526, he drew on the same stock of tales that Rastell had used for his original edition, 'A', but offered a different selection, which implies that the manuscript commonplace book from which the tales were drawn was in Rastell's possession at the time, and the most probable reason for this is that it was Rastell's own work.

Had the tales been the work of anyone other than Rastell, it is difficult to imagine how an alternative selection of the same tales could have been offered: any other author would surely have submitted a manuscript of the tales as he hoped to see them published, rather than submitting a larger collection with a vague instruction to choose the hundred merriest. By contrast, it is easy to see how if Rastell, working from his own manuscript, had prepared the first edition, 'A', by selecting the tales as he went along, an element of confusion might have occurred when he asked a third party, Peter Treveris, to prepare a new edition from the same source. After Treveris had offered a different selection of tales for the second edition, 'B', it must surely have been Rastell who saw to it that later editions would follow his original conception for the book, perhaps dropping Tale 100 as well as two of the tales introduced by Treveris, and restoring the final tales from his own first edition, 'A'.

It also seems significant that Rastell did not attribute *A Hundred Merry Tales* to another author. If Rastell had been indebted to another writer for the work, he would usually have credited them, as he did with, for example, *The Mery Gestys of the Widow Edith*, published in 1525, which he acknowledged as the work of Walter Smith, a servant of Sir Thomas More. If however Rastell had reworked anecdotes which were drawn from a variety of sources, he may have been wary of claiming the authorship for himself.

Taken together, these factors strongly indicate that the original manuscript source for the *Tales* was compiled by John Rastell himself and, as the tales are all stylistically similar, that rather than being copied *verbatim* from written sources, the manuscript retold each anecdote in Rastell's own words. Thus, it seems most likely that the *Hundred Merry Tales* were not only printed but also compiled by John Rastell, and it is very probably his own legalistic style in which the tales are set down—and, although Rastell's style may indeed be 'ponderous' and 'diffuse', it is also engaging, conversational and unpretentious, savouring the essential wit of each story without unnecessary embellishment.

In this sense, we may consider Rastell to be the author of *A Hundred Merry Tales*, but this is not to suggest that he invented any of the individual anecdotes himself. Although many of the tales have no known source, a large number of those without literary antecedents may have been picked up orally, as were Poggio's *facetiae*, while others may have reached Rastell in letters from friends or through lost manuscript sources. If so, given this mixed background, it is not at all surprising that Rastell did not set his own name as author to the collection. However, it makes sense for us now to recognise John Rastell as effective author of the body of tales as a whole.

Who was John Rastell?

In his lifetime, John Rastell was an adventurer and explorer, he worked as an artist alongside Holbein, he wrote entertainments for kings and emperors, he created the first usable type for printing music, he was the first printer of secular drama, and he built the first modern theatre, but it is on his legacy as a writer, printer and publisher, most importantly as a publisher of legal works, that his reputation now chiefly rests. Rastell's legal writings both codified the law and translated it into English, and their publication in printed form brought a knowledge and understanding of English law within the grasp of ordinary people for the first time in history.

There is no doubt that Rastell set about his work of writing and printing books of law in the hopes of creating a better world: he wrote that 'the common weal by all reason must rather stand in augmenting and preferring of laws than either in riches, power or honour, so they that exercise and busy themself in making laws and writing of laws, in learning laws or teaching of laws, or in just and true executing of laws, be those persons that greatly increase and multiply the common weal' (*Liber Assisarum*, c.1514), and that 'the craft of printing of books … hath been cause of great learning and knowledge, and hath been the cause of many things and great changes, and is like to be the cause of many strange things hereafter to come' (*The Pastime of People*, 1529).

The following brief account of Rastell's life draws chiefly on the seminal biography of John Rastell in A. W. Reed's *Early Tudor Drama* (1926, Ch.1 and Appendices 1-8), and on a more recent discussion in the Introduction to Devereux's *Bibliography* (1999).

John Rastell was born in Coventry, probably in 1475, the son of Thomas Rastell J.P. and his wife Elizabeth. He was married, perhaps in 1497, to Elizabeth More (1482-1537), daughter of London lawyer Sir

John More and sister of Sir Thomas More, through whom he was introduced to the circle of early English humanists. John and Elizabeth Rastell had three children together, Joan, John and William. Rastell pursued a career in law and, in 1502, he appears as an 'utter barrister' (junior barrister) in the records of Middle Temple, London.

From 1506 until 1508, Rastell was once more in Coventry after succeeding his father as Coroner—Sir Thomas More visited him there at around this time, and wrote of his encounter with a preaching friar in the city. Coventry was a hotbed of Lollardy and, in 1507, Rastell was named as overseer in the will of an ex-mayor whose bequests included a 'bible in English'. In 1509 however, perhaps inspired by the accession of the young humanist Prince Henry as king of England, Rastell moved back to London, working not only as a lawyer but also as a printer and publisher 'at the Fleet Bridge at the Abbot of Winchcombe's Place'. Among the first books published by Rastell was *The Life of Johan Picus*, his brother-in-law's translation of a biography by Gianfrancesco Pico.

Through the patronage of Coventry-born courtier Sir Edward Belknap, Rastell was employed during the French war of 1512-14 as an engineer responsible for artillery transport. Around this time, Rastell also took new premises near St Paul's for his printing press, which included a shop as well as living quarters. In 1515, after his return from France, Rastell was able to afford the lease on a country house with large gardens at Monken Hadley, near High Barnet.

Later that year, Belknap secured wardship for Rastell of the two daughters of the condemned heretic Richard Hunne. Hunne's treatment by the Church was a notorious scandal which helped foster anti-clericalism in London but, for Rastell personally, the wardship was also a lucrative windfall whereby he received all of Hunne's lands and goods. Through his wards, Rastell might also have encountered at first hand some of the thinking of religious radicals like Hunne.

In 1517, Rastell led an expedition to search for a western route to Asia and to colonise the New World. The trip was supported by Henry VIII and was partly funded by Sir Edward Howard, Lord High Admiral, but ended in mutiny on the Irish coast, where his crew 'exhorted the said Rastell ... to give up his voyage and to fall to robbing upon the sea' (Court of Requests, 15 November 1519, Req.2/3/192; see Reed p.187-201). Rastell was stranded in Waterford while his ships sailed on for France, but he used the opportunity to write a moral play called *A New Interlude and a Merry of the Nature of the Four Elements*, which he published on his return in 1519 from a new print shop at St Paul's Gate, Cheapside.

Through the patronage of Sir Edward Belknap, Rastell was appointed in 1520 to paint the ceilings for the celebrated royal pavilion at the Field of the Cloth of Gold and for the Round House in Calais, and in 1522, he wrote and choreographed the pageants performed in London for the king's meeting with Emperor Charles V. At around this time, Rastell's daughter Joan married the court musician John Heywood who would later find fame as a playwright and epigrammatist—through the Heywoods' daughter Elizabeth, Rastell would one day become the great grandfather of the poet John Donne.

As part of the terms of his wardship of the daughters of Richard Hunne, Rastell was obliged to pay their dowries to the Crown but he defaulted in May 1523, and Hunne's property was re-granted to another. Rastell challenged this decision in court, so it would not be until 1529 that he would finally lose the benefit of Hunne's lands.

In 1524, Rastell took out a lease on land at Finsbury Fields where he built a new house so that, in 1524-5, when *A Hundred Merry Tales* was published, John Rastell was living as a prosperous and respected humanist lawyer and printer, well-connected with friends at court, with houses at Monken Hadley and Finsbury Fields, and premises at Paul's Gate, Cheapside, where his printing shop was ably run by the professional printer Thomas Kele.

By 1527 Rastell's new home at Finsbury Fields was also the site of the first dedicated public theatre in the modern world. This new theatre may have been the same structure which Rastell had worked on with Holbein for the king's pageants at Greenwich. Rastell had not only embellished the theatre, but had written and directed entertainments for these pageants, and he may simply have ordered the carpenter Henry Walton to re-erect the same stage at his house.

Probably through the agency of his brother-in-law Sir Thomas More, Rastell was returned as M.P. in the Reformation Parliament of 1529 for the Cornish borough of Dunheved, and the same year he spent six months in France on government business, where he was probably seeking support from the academics of Paris University for the king's divorce. Also in 1529, Rastell printed Sir Thomas More's *Dialogue Concerning Heresies*, which attacked the works of Martin Luther and William Tyndale, and affirmed the validity of the authority, traditions and practices of the Church. Rastell was moved to join the debate alongside his brother-in-law, writing and printing *A New Book of Purgatory* in 1530.

Unlike More however, Rastell's first loyalty was not to the authority of the Catholic Church but to his conception of Justice and Natural Law. Thus by 1532 he was a convert to the new religion, and henceforth, John Rastell's printing press would serve the Protestant Reformation, while his son William and his brother-in-law Sir Thomas More redoubled their efforts in support of the Papacy. As Rastell grew apart from More, so he drew closer to Thomas Cromwell. He was employed to print statutes for the first session of the Reformation Parliament, was considered as a possible Master of Christ Church Priory, Aldgate, and may have been appointed to supervise legal instruments within the City of London. Cromwell also involved Rastell in an unsuccessful attempt at lead mining on Dartmoor.

From this time on however, Rastell's obsession with religious and political reform would lead him to neglect his own affairs and, after 1532, he seems to have entrusted his printing business entirely to his teenage apprentice William Mayhewe. Lawsuits also now began to catch up with Rastell: having lost the Hunne wardship in 1529, in 1534 he lost his house in Monken Hadley through a legal dispute with his mother-in-law, Dame Alice More, and brother-in-law, Richard Staverton; in the same year, Rastell was also involved in a court case regarding his printing premises in St Paul's Gate, Cheapside.

In 1534, Rastell approached Cromwell with a plan for a new printing project called *The Book of the Charge*, to be read at courts and assizes, 'whereby not only the learned men themself but also the people shall be instructed in true learning, and brought from ignorance to knowledge of the true faith, and to have no confidence in the pope.' The first copy of the printed book was apparently sent back by Cromwell for revision and, in a long letter of response, Rastell asks for ten or twelve days leisure to complete the task, continuing with a frank statement of the difficulties he faced:

> ... it is not unknown to you that I have spent my time and given my business principally this four or five years in compiling diverse books concerning the furtherance of the king's causes and opposing of the pope's usurped authority, and thereby greatly hindered mine own business that, as I shall answer afore God, I am the worse for it by a hundred pounds and above, and beside that, I have decayed the trade of my living, for where before that, I got by the law in pleading in Westminster Hall forty mark a year (that was twenty nobles a term, at the least) and printed every year two or three hundred ream of paper which was more yearly profit to me than the gains that I got by the law, I assure you I get not now forty shillings a year by the law, nor I printed not a hundred ream of paper this two year ...

I am an old man—I look not to live long and I regard riches as much as I do [wood]chips, save only to have a living to live out of debt, and I care as much for worldly honour as I care for the flying of a feather in the wind, but I desire most so to spend my time to do somewhat for the common wealth, as God be my judge . . .

Therefore, if the king's grace would do the cost to print four or five thousand and give them among the people, which would not cost above a hundred pounds, it would turn the minds of the people and bring them to the right belief, and do as much good as the preachings do.

In 1535, Rastell was outspoken in his objection to the continued levy of tithes by the Church of England, which he believed were an intolerable burden on the poorest in society and allowed the rich to put off their charitable duties. Either because of his opposition to tithes or because he was a debtor to the Crown, Rastell was arrested and imprisoned. In a last letter to his capricious benefactor Cromwell, he describes himself as 'a poor prisoner, bewrapped with care, thought and heaviness, perturbed with languor, sorrow and pensiveness, oppressed with extreme poverty, and now by long imprisonment brought to extreme misery, forsaken of my kinsmen, destitute of my friends, aidless, comfortless and succourless . . .'

On 25th June 1536, Rastell was dead. There is a tragic irony that the man who had striven harder than anyone to celebrate the value of law, and to bring an understanding of English law to ordinary people, should have died in prison where, like the prisoner in Tale 98, he was held indefinitely without trial and without any prospect of release.

The Tales in their Sixteenth-century Context

For nineteenth-century critics, *A Hundred Merry Tales* was 'characterized by little respect to delicacy of speech or regard for decency of manners' (Singer, 1815) and was 'a coarse book, the natural product of coarse times' (Furness, 1899). These comments now seem to tell us more about the critics than they do about the *Tales*. As modern readers, we too bring our own perspectives to Rastell's *Merry Tales*, but old texts also offer us an opportunity to understand earlier perspectives on the world.

So, what would the *Tales* have meant to sixteenth century readers?

The *Tales* tend to approach comedy not so much as an end in itself, but as a way to reveal insights about the nature of humanity. Several stories raise themes of anti-clericalism and misogyny, while tales of Welshmen raise the spectre of xenophobia. References to the *Tales* by sixteenth-century writers including Shakespeare also help us to understand earlier perspectives on the book, and how it came to be regarded as a classic.

Attitudes towards the Welsh

The horizons of the English in 1524-5 were more limited than those of later centuries, and so early Tudor xenophobia was directed principally at people from other parts of Britain and Ireland. There are tales which mock the Irish (Tale 13), the Scots (Tale 61) and the northern English (Tale 99), but the main target is undoubtedly the Welsh. Prejudice against the Welsh has been a recurrent feature of English xenophobia, and to some extent, it continues to this day. For the Tudor readership of *A Hundred Merry Tales*, Welsh servants were evidently a familiar aspect of daily life, and may have provoked similar insecurities to immigrants today.

There may have been an accentuated interest in 'Welsh jokes' in early Tudor England, reflecting English insecurities about their Welsh monarch after the accession of Henry Tudor to the English throne in 1485. At the close of the Tudor era, the accession of the first Scottish king of England would certainly prompt a flurry of 'Scottish jokes' in plays such as *Eastward Ho!* and *The Isle of Gulls*. By 1524-5 however, the Tudor dynasty was already well-established; Henry VIII had been born and brought up as an English prince, and there is no special political element to the portrayal of the Welsh in *A Hundred Merry Tales*. Welshmen in the *Tales* are mostly servants, and this is a pattern of immigration which is unlikely to have altered significantly in 1485.

Many landholders in late medieval Wales were English, and service to an English lord was no doubt an attractive possibility for an aspiring Welsh youth. The Welshmen we meet in the *Merry Tales* are usually personal retainers, but Welshmen had long been familiar at all levels of English society and, in 1400, Welsh labourers in England had been notable among the supporters of Owain Glyndŵr. It is not difficult to imagine how the English regarded an immigrant population of poor foreign workers speaking broken English, and here the Welsh servant is mocked for his foreign accent and his poor understanding of English (which he would have learned as a second language).

In Tales 16 and 30, we meet the Welshman in his native land, where he appears to live without regard for life or laws. Rightly or wrongly, the lawlessness of Wales is a recurring theme in sixteenth-century English sources. In 1534, several years after the publication of *A Hundred Merry Tales*, Thomas Cromwell would appoint Rastell to the service of Bishop Roland Lee, Lord President of the Council of Wales and the Marches. Bishop Lee's operation in Wales has been variously described as a 'commission investigating lawlessness in Wales' and as a 'reign of terror', but Rastell, untiring champion that he was of the law as the instrument of the common good, would undoubtedly have considered he was helping to establish the rule of law.

Rastell clearly enjoyed a joke at the expense of the Welsh and it is difficult not to view this as an instance of anti-Welsh prejudice, but the jokes against Welshmen in *A Hundred Merry Tales* are not especially savage—there is certainly nothing in the Tudor editions to compare with William Carew Hazlitt's direct assault on the Welsh character in his 1887 edition (p.20). And just as Rastell's *Merry Tales* mock the Welsh for their difficulties with the English language, so in Wales, English lack of understanding of the Welsh language provided a source of merriment for poets such as Tudur Penllyn (*fl. c.*1420–90).

The stereotypical Welshman of *A Hundred Merry Tales* is characterised as literal-minded and hot-tempered, naturally violent, with scant regard for the rule of law, given to swearing, and addicted to hot cheese (which suggests not only a national dish, but also a lack of moderation) but, as with Shakespeare's Fluellen, 'There is much care and valour in this Welshman.' The Welsh servant is unswervingly loyal, and it is in the particular combination of loyalty and misunderstanding that much of the humour lies in the *Merry Tales*. Above all, the Welshman in caricature is recognisable by his thick accent, his failure to understand the niceties of sixteenth-century English, and his literal mindedness, which may reveal as much about English attitudes towards foreigners as about the Welsh themselves.

Moral mirth

For Rastell, comedy was not an end in itself. His intention was to use humour to serve a higher purpose, directing his readers towards virtue and upright behaviour. In this respect, Rastell's *Merry Tales* may be compared to his other works dedicated to supporting the common weal. In *A Hundred Merry Tales*, the moral purpose is made explicit in the explanatory moral tags which are appended to most of the tales.

The precepts of the moral tags are sometimes more a matter of practical advice than higher morality, but they usually direct the reader towards sensible and respectable conduct in an orderly, law-abiding society. We read 'that one ought to take heed how he rebuketh another lest it turn most to his own rebuke' (Tales 14 and 60), or that 'it is folly for a man to say 'yea' or 'nay' to a matter except he know surely what the matter is' (Tale 51). In small group of consecutive tales (Tales 54, 55, 56, 57), the tags remind the reader that a Latin prayer has been rendered into English for 'they that be unlearned in the Latin tongue'. At other times, the tags take aim against pomposity and hypocrisy, against foolish speech, and all the many ways in which we can make fools of ourselves through our folly and vanity.

A similar combination of merriment and morality is seen in Rastell's earlier work, *The Four Elements* (1519), where his Messenger explains:

> ...because some folk be little disposed
> To sadness, but more to mirth and sport,
> This philosophical work is mixed
> With merry conceits, to give men comfort
> And occasion to cause them to resort
> To hear this matter, whereto if they take heed
> Some learning to them thereof may proceed.

(134-40)

Likewise, in Henry Medwall's play *Fulgens and Lucrece* (c.1497), which was printed by Rastell in 1512-16, Medwall expresses his intention:

> Not only to make folk mirth and game,
> But that such as be gentlemen of name
> May be somewhat moved
> By this example for to eschew
> The way of vice, and favour virtue ...

(*Fulgens and Lucrece*, II, 890-4)

When Robert Langham mentions *A Hundred Merry Tales* in his letter of 1575 (published 1580) among the books supposedly in the library of the fictional duelling mason and Coventrian, Captain Cox, it is listed under the heading of 'Philosophy, both moral and natural.' Although the absurdity of this filing error was surely meant as a jest in itself, it acknowledges the pedagogical moral purpose of the *Tales*, and suggests that, for the likes of Captain Cox, such moral jests may have been the limit of their philosophical education—by contrast, the *Tales* are placed among 'infortunate treatises and amorous toys written in English' by Meredith Hanmer in the dedication to his translation of Eusebius (1577).

In our own day, the notion of moral comedy may seem unfamiliar, and modern attitudes towards prescriptive morality can make it feel awkward, but comedy can still be turned to serious ends in political satire, and this satirical approach is mirrored most closely in Rastell's anti-clerical tales. The combination of comedy with morality in *A Hundred Merry Tales* is not consistently successful and, as modern readers, we might not laugh at every anecdote, but contemporaries would have been better able to appreciate the moral and satirical aspects of the *Tales*, which would have remained in their minds as memorable exemplars to consider in their daily lives.

Anti-clericalism

Roughly a quarter of the *Merry Tales* are directed against the corruption, greed and ineptitude of contemporary churchmen. In Rastell's England, matters of Church and religion occupied a similar place to that of secular politics today. Religious dissent was most clearly expressed in the Lollards, who had emerged in the fourteenth century as followers of the preacher and theologian John Wycliffe (d.1384). Their *Twelve Conclusions of the Lollards*, which had been nailed to the doors of

Westminster Abbey and St Paul's Cathedral in 1395, questioned the authority of the priesthood and its involvement in secular affairs, condemned exorcism, confession, pilgrimage, and the doctrine of transubstantiation, along with clerical celibacy, the practice of paying priests to sing prayers for specific people, and the justification of war on grounds of religion.

Many of the themes of the anti-clericalism which grew throughout the fifteenth and sixteenth centuries reflect concerns raised in the *Conclusions of the Lollards*, and these complaints against the clergy were already well-established when Martin Luther's *Ninety-five Theses* transformed the religious landscape in 1517. By no means everyone who enjoyed anti-clerical stories was a Lollard or a Protestant, but the reason the ignorant priest, the lascivious and gluttonous friar and the avaricious monk became stock characters in popular stories is that they exemplify the recognised abuses of the late medieval Church.

Rastell would ultimately come to accept the arguments of the Protestant reformers, but at the time the *Merry Tales* was published in 1524–5, he remained loyal to the traditions of the English Church supported by royal and papal authority as they had endured for centuries. In 1521, Pope Leo X had granted King Henry VIII the title *Fidei defensor* ('Defender of the Faith') for his book *Assertio Septem Sacramentorum* ('Assertion of the Seven Sacraments'); the next year, Luther had replied with *Contra Henricum Regem Anglie* ('Against Henry, King of the English') and, in 1523, Rastell's brother-in-law Sir Thomas More returned fire with his *Responsio ad Lutherum* ('Response to Luther'). The debate between Lutherans and Catholics continued with tract and counter-tract, and in 1530 Rastell himself would pitch in against the Lutherans with *A New Book of Purgatory*. So, although the *Tales* can be sharply critical of clerical malpractice, it would be a mistake to confuse this with the zeal of Protestant Reformation.

Nevertheless, Rastell and More were part of a humanist circle which openly condemned clerical abuses, and Rastell may also have encountered Lollardy directly during his time as Coroner in Coventry in 1506-8, and again through the daughters of Richard Hunne after 1515. Several tales tackle themes which feed into the prevailing mood of scepticism towards the clergy: some tales are obviously critical; others undermine clerical authority by portraying practices such as confession in the context of an absurd scenario; even Tale 22 'Of the merchant that charged his son to find one to sing for his soul,' which does not mention the clergy directly, can be better understood in the light of the controversy over the singing of prayers for the dead. Mendicant friars come in for particularly broad criticism, but whenever the *Tales* tackle other clergy, they are careful to limit any criticism to specific abuses, so whilst it is hard to avoid the feeling that too many parish priests were poorly educated, the institution of the priesthood and the hierarchy of the Church are not in themselves subject to criticism .

In poking fun at the abuses of the Church, the *Hundred Merry Tales* was giving vent to sentiments which were already widely held, and some tales may have long been told in taverns and on street corners. It is one thing though to tell jokes about greedy friars over a drink, but quite another to print and publish a collection of such tales in English. Part of the initial popularity of *A Hundred Merry Tales* may have derived from the *frisson* of reading in print what everyone was saying in private. That this was permissible in 1524-5 is a testament to the relaxed confidence of the young Catholic humanist monarch, Henry VIII.

All too soon however, the merry mood would change. In 1530, amidst the turmoil of 'the King's Great Matter,' Rastell's brother-in-law Sir Thomas More would succeed Cardinal Thomas Wolsey as Lord Chancellor, maintaining measures to prevent the spread of Lutheran literature in England through far-reaching censorship laws and an

Index of forbidden books. Then, with little warning, the tide would turn against More. In 1531, Henry VIII purged the senior English clergy, and in November 1534, he was appointed as Supreme Head of the Church of England. Unable to accept the king's supremacy in religion, Sir Thomas More would be executed within the year. From this perspective, *A Hundred Merry Tales* represents a brief comic flowering before the brewing storm.

Misogyny

If anti-clericalism was a concern of the sixteenth century which seems less urgent to us today, the opposite is true of misogyny. Medieval society was founded on the assumption that different roles were played by men and women, and that the domestic work performed by women was a real and essential labour upon which their menfolk depended. As a result, the relationship between the sexes was necessarily different. Certainly, some women of the time regarded their work as mere drudgery, but some male occupations were equal in drudgery.

This stronger separation of gender roles did not stem solely from contemporary domestic arrangements. Marriage was a holy sacrament bestowed by the Church, which assigned clearly defined roles to husband and wife. Although religious ceremonies were conducted in Latin, ordinary people were expected to understand the significance of Latin texts even if they did not understand the language, and, according to the wedding ceremony, it was the man's role to 'keep and protect' his wife (*tenere et custodire*), while it was the woman's role to 'serve and obey' her husband (*obedire et servire*).

For men and women in early Tudor England, the separation of gender roles was simply a matter of fact, but there was inevitably a rivalry between the sexes, which expressed itself in popular literature of the time, and it may have been possible for both men and women to be more relaxed about what could be perceived as sexist humour, because of their acceptance of the different roles allotted by society. In view of this, we should not be surprised to discover that several of the *Tales* express blatant misogyny, which can be seen most clearly in Tales 9, 21, 62, 63, 86 and 102. These tales however do not seem to represent a deliberately misogynistic agenda, but merely trot out a conventional opinion as the basis for a joke. With the partial exception of the fantastical Tale 62, misogynistic sentiment in these tales is limited to relaying a comment exchanged between male characters; they reflect an established male attitude towards women which, whatever the effect of promulgating such attitudes, could have been adopted for the sake of humour without real malicious intent.

Tales 34 and 35 raise the spectre of domestic abuse, and modern readers may be appalled that this could ever have been considered a subject for humour. However, a closer reading reveals a less problematic treatment of the subject. In each case, the husband makes what he believes to be an empty threat; in the first tale, the franklin imagines that his threatened violence will so horrify the friar that his unwanted guest will leave, while in the second tale, the poor man hopes to use the presence of a guest to nullify his threat. The joke in both tales relies on our shock that the husband is willing to be regarded as a wife-beater to avoid a more trivial social embarrassment. This shock is reinforced by the realisation that the friar, who ought to represent a higher morality, seems unconcerned by the husband's threatened violence, which in turn undermines our confidence in the authority of friars. Thus, the structure of the joke relies on the expectation that readers will regard domestic violence with distaste or even horror. That this is not a situation of genuine danger (and thus may be an acceptable situation for humour) is underlined in Tale 35 by the reaction of the wife, who is not at all frightened of her husband, but is justly annoyed at the disgraceful behaviour of the two men at her table.

Many of the *Hundred Merry Tales* do focus on the relationship between the sexes but, although some tales do indeed seem to be straightforwardly misogynistic (perhaps most blatantly in the moral to Tale 10), the dynamic in the collection as a whole is more finely balanced. Women may not be safe from ridicule and criticism in the *Tales* but, in a collection where no one gets off unscathed, there seems to be no deliberate misogynistic agenda. Sometimes male characters in the tales do exemplify outright misogyny, but they usually make fools of themselves as a result, as in Tale 66 'Of the man that would have the pot stand there as he would.' Even in a tale such as 'Of him that said that a woman's tongue was lightest meat of digestion' (Tale 9), where an overtly misogynistic remark forms the basis of a joke, this is not real animosity, but light-hearted banter within a well-established framework—there is no reason to imagine the man genuinely believes what he says, and the humour here is directed against the physician rather than the man's wife.

In other tales, a man may be outwitted in sexist banter by a woman. Women in the *Tales* frequently succeed in turning the tables on their male antagonists whereas, by contrast, there is not a single tale where a man finds an apt riposte to a woman. If the *Tales* had a misogynistic agenda, these female triumphs would be portrayed as an absurd or disturbing inversion of the natural order but instead, whenever the woman gets one over on the man, we are invited as readers to share in the joke without regard to our own gender. So, whilst these tales acknowledge that, in the thorough-goingly patriarchal society of sixteenth-century England, misogyny is commonplace among men, they relish the woman's witty riposte rather than the man's attempted scorn. In the context of the prevailing patriarchy, they represent the victory of the underdog, and both male and female readers alike share a delight in seeing these witty women triumph over their conceited opponents.

In a society that could often be genuinely misogynistic, it is remarkable that this group of tales appears to be actively engaged in challenging the sexist attitudes which were rife among contemporaries; examples can be found in Tales 20, 23, 29, 32, 49, 58, 66 and 103. Although the repeated tag-line that 'a woman's answer is never to seek' assumes a male perspective, it is also, despite its overtones of implicit patriarchal chauvinism, an admission that women can be relied on to hold their own. Such stories allowed readers to explore undercurrents of an alternative relationship between the sexes, which they must have recognised from their own lives, but which were at odds with the norms represented in the institutions of sixteenth-century society. The message to women in this group of tales is clearly that they can be more than a match for any man, if they so wish.

This aspect of the *Tales* does not make Rastell a proto-feminist any more than his misogynistic tales make him an anti-feminist. But the fact that misogyny is robustly addressed and ridiculed in several tales is nonetheless significant, and may have been more obvious to contemporaries than it is to modern readers. Indeed, there is some evidence that, for Shakespeare and his audience, *A Hundred Merry Tales* was a byword for witty, outspoken women.

The Shakespeare jest book

In Shakespeare's *Much Ado about Nothing* (II.i.), Beatrice remarks that she has heard it said, 'That I was disdainful, and that I had my good wit out of the *Hundred Merry Tales*:—well, this was Signior Benedick that said so.'

There has been some confusion over the significance of this reference. Nineteenth-century critics, who despised *A Hundred Merry Tales* for its coarseness and indelicacy, unhesitatingly assumed that their idol Shakespeare would have shared their own prejudices.

Thus, according to Singer, 'the manner in which it is mentioned by Shakespeare, manifests the contempt he entertained for it' (p.xi), while Furness, after roundly condemning *A Hundred Merry Tales* as 'not unlike the atmosphere of the houses which demanded daily and prolonged fumigations,' remarked, 'Well, indeed, may Beatrice have deeply resented the imputation that from it she drew her wit' (Furness 1899, p.72). Furness is then duly amazed that the same book had been 'the solace of Queen Elizabeth's dying hours.' But if *A Hundred Merry Tales* could be suitable reading for a sixteenth-century queen, it is clear that these nineteenth-century critics, blinded by their own narrow cultural values, were missing the point.

In fact, *A Hundred Merry Tales* was by no means despised by Shakespeare's contemporaries. First published more than seventy years before *Much Ado* was written (probably in 1598-9), the *Merry Tales* would remain in print into the next century and, as late as 1622, would be cited by Taylor the Water Poet in his *Sir Gregory Nonsense*. Shakespeare was referring to an old classic, which he knew was both familiar to his audience and well-loved. So, what is the real reason that Shakespeare refers to Rastell's work?

By the start of Act II, when this reference occurs, the character of Beatrice and her relationship with Benedick is sufficiently well established for the audience to recognise parallels in popular literature. Partly because such spirited women are rarely portrayed in earlier literature, the similarity of Shakespeare's Beatrice to the witty women of the *Tales*, in particular in Tale 29 'Of the gentleman that wished his tooth in the gentlewoman's tail' (which is also alluded to by Shakespeare in *The Taming of the Shrew*, see p.133) and Tale 32 'Of the gentlewoman that said to a gentleman, "Ye have a beard above and none beneath"', are striking. Contemporary play-goers would doubtless have recognised how apposite this reference was to *A Hundred Merry Tales* in a way that has eluded more recent scholars.

Benedick's accusation that Beatrice had her 'good wit out of the *Hundred Merry Tales*' does not criticise the supposed source of her wit—the criticism she rejects so strongly is that she might simply be re-hashing old jokes. But perhaps there is a grain of truth in Benedick's ungallant remark. Whilst Beatrice's own wit is undoubtedly spontaneous and genuine, Shakespeare may well have drawn inspiration for her character and for the 'merry war betwixt Signior Benedick and her' (I.i.) directly from the merry war between the sexes in *A Hundred Merry Tales*. Likewise, the bumbling Dogberry and his companions may have been inspired by the absurd malapropisms of the yokel husbandman in Tale 7, 'Of the husbandman that asked for Master Pisspot the Physician.'

So, far from sneering at it, Shakespeare deliberately name-checks *A Hundred Merry Tales* because, for his contemporaries, the themes of his play will have already brought the book to mind. By explicitly referring to his inspiration, he subtly deflects any potential criticism from would-be Benedicks in the audience who might otherwise have claimed that Shakespeare's own wit was just a re-hash of Rastell's work. If earlier generations of commentators missed this connection, it may be partly because they were unable or unwilling to recognise the strengths of *A Hundred Merry Tales* which appealed to contemporary readers, and partly because they were too eager to regard Shakespeare as a purely original genius without acknowledging his inevitable debt to earlier writers.

The influence of *A Hundred Merry Tales* extends to other plays including *The Taming of the Shrew* and, more generally, to the worlds of Bottom and the Mechanicals in *A Midsummer Night's Dream*, and Falstaff and his cronies in *Henry IV, Parts I & II* and *The Merry Wives of Windsor*. Most modern critics rank *The Merry Wives* among Shakespeare's least successful works, and it may have been written at a time when a rift was growing between Shakespeare and the clown Will Kemp, which is associated with Shakespeare's rejection of the 'merry' approach to comedy. The humour of later Shakespearian fools has as little in common with the rumbustious spirit of *A Hundred Merry Tales* as it has with his own earlier comedies, but this does not negate the apparent influence of the *Merry Tales* on his earlier work.

The invention of Merry England

There is a surprisingly large number of direct references to *A Hundred Merry Tales* from the later sixteenth and early seventeenth centuries. Citations in Hanmer's *Eusebius* (1577), the Langham Letter (1580), Shakespeare's *Much Ado* (1598-9) and Taylor's *Sir Gregory Nonsense* (1622), have been noted, as well as its favour with Queen Elizabeth in her dying days (1603). The book is also mentioned by name in *Civil and Uncivil Life* (1579), Bathe's *Introduction to the Art of Musick* (1584), Fulke's *Apology against the railing Declamation of Peter Frarine* (1586), Lyly's *Pap with an Hatchet* (1589), Harvey's *Pierce's Supererogation* (1593), Dekker's *Wonderful Year* (1603), *Willy Beguiled* (1606) and Gataker's *The popish Doctrine of Transubstantiation* (1624), as well as in a note to Harington's *Metamorphosis of Ajax* (1596) where it seems an anecdote from an altogether different jest book has been mistakenly attributed to the more familiar *Hundred Merry Tales*. This is an impressively large list of citations, centring on the 1590's. Thus, by the end of the sixteenth century, *A Hundred Merry Tales* was apparently regarded as a classic, and may indeed have been enjoying a resurgence in popularity.

What could account for the growing popularity of the *Tales* in Shakespearian England, seventy years after their first publication? Part of the answer may be simply that *A Hundred Merry Tales* was recognised as the first of its kind, as the model for all the many jest books that were to follow, but this does not seem sufficient in itself to explain the renewed interest the book attracted in the reign of Elizabeth I. There was however one particular factor which gave the tales a special resonance for readers in the later sixteenth century.

Then, as now, *A Hundred Merry Tales* offered a fascinating glimpse of an England on the brink of the Reformation—its characters inhabit a world which had resolved the century of dynastic warfare immortalised by Shakespeare as the 'Wars of the Roses', and are engagingly unaware of the social and religious upheavals which would define the century to come. After the publication of the *Tales* in 1524-5, England underwent a traumatic series of religious changes, veering from fully-fledged Protestantism under Edward VI (1547-53) to the persecution of Protestants under his sister Mary (1553-8).

When Elizabeth came to the throne in 1558, she tried to accommodate both Catholic and Protestant subjects, declaring, 'There is only one Christ, Jesus, one faith—all else is a dispute over trifles,' and she insisted on a more moderate form of religion than had been practised under her brother Edward VI. Despite this, the religious divide dramatically re-opened in 1569 with the Rebellion of the Northern Earls, which aimed to restore Catholicism and to depose Elizabeth in favour of Mary Queen of Scots. The next year, Pope Pius V issued the Bull, *Regnans in Excelsis*, which excommunicated 'Elizabeth, the pretended queen of England', and commanded all Catholics to disobey her laws or be excommunicated along with their queen. Elizabeth's excommunication precipitated a series of plots to depose the queen and restore Catholicism, backed by foreign military might. Despite Elizabeth's attempt to straddle the religious divide, it had become the single most important issue of her reign, and recusant Catholics across the country were automatically under suspicion of treason.

Although Elizabethan England was riven by tensions between Catholics and Protestants, many ordinary people had little interest in the religious arguments of the day. If they were content to be Protestant under Elizabeth, they would have been more content had such divisions never turned one Englishman against another. It is scarcely any wonder if they harked back nostalgically to an idealised vision of England before the Reformation. This fantasy could be indulged through Rastell's *Hundred Merry Tales*.

Whatever the true nature of English society in the mid-1520's, a shallowly nostalgic reading of *A Hundred Merry Tales* can suggest a society utterly at ease with itself, where happy people from all walks of life engaged in light-hearted buffoonery. Although the issues tackled by the *Merry Tales* had been significant at the time, later generations would see its tales of fat friars and Latin-speaking priests as reflections of a simpler, happier world, which their grandparents had known. Thus, it was not merely the merriment of the *Tales* which delighted later readers, but also the fact that it brought life to a past that seemed in retrospect to be a lost idyll. In the world of *A Hundred Merry Tales*, they found a merry England, a brief Golden Age which lay between the dynastic divisions of the Wars of the Roses and the religious divisions of the Reformation.

THE TALES

1. Of him that said there were but two commandments.

A CERTAIN curate in the country there was, that preached in the pulpit of the Ten Commandments, saying that there were Ten Commandments that every man ought to keep, and he that broke any of them committed grievous sin. Howbeit, he said that sometime it was deadly sin and sometime venial, but when it was deadly sin and when venial there were many doubts therein.

And a miller, a young man, a mad fellow that came seldom to church and had been at very few sermons or none in all his life, answered him then shortly this wise:

'I marvel, Master Parson, that ye say there be so many commandments and so many doubts. For I never heard tell but of two commandments, that is to say "Commend me to you," and "Commend me from you." Nor I never heard tell of more doubts but twain, that is to say "D'out the candle," and "D'out the fire."'

At which answer, all the people fell a-laughing.

By this tale a man may well perceive that they that be brought up without learning or good manner shall never be but rude and beastly although they have good natural wits.

curate: a priest charged with the cure or care of souls, a parish priest (1).

deadly sin: a mortal sin, considered serious enough to send the sinner to Hell (6-7).

venial sin: an ordinary or less serious sin (6-7).

mad: wild, irrational, harebrained (9).

shortly: promptly, hastily (11).

"Commend me to you," and *"Commend me from you":* the young miller has deliberately confused the word 'command' with 'commend' (14-5).

"D'out the candle," and *"D'out the fire":* here the young miller is confusing the word 'doubt' with 'do out'—to do out the candle or fire, is to quench it or put it out (16-7).

a-laughing: to laughing; literally 'on laughing' (18).

rude: uneducated, uncouth (21).

beastly: bestial, like a beast or animal (21).

The moral is among several which contrast wisdom, learning and orderly behaviour with foolishness, wilfulness and stupidity, *cf.* Tales 5, 8, 34, 37, 67, 69, 71, 73, 75 and 81.

2. Of the citizen that called the priest 'Sir John,' and he called him 'Master Ralph.'

ON A TIME there was a jolly citizen walking in the country for sport, which met with a foolish priest and in derision in communication called him 'Sir John.' This priest, understanding his mocking, called him
5   'Master Ralph.'

'Why,' quod the citizen, 'dost thou call me Master Ralph?'

'Marry,' quod the priest, 'why callest me Sir John?'

Then quod the citizen, 'I call thee Sir John because
10   every foolish priest most commonly is called Sir John.'

'Marry,' quod the priest, 'and I call thee Master Ralph because every proud cuckold most commonly is called Master Ralph!'

At the which answer all that were by laughed apace,
15   because diverse there supposed the same citizen to be a cuckold indeed.

By this tale ye may see that he that delighteth to deride and laugh other to scorn is sometime himself more derided.

B.2: *Of the cytisen that callyd the prest syr John & he callyd him master raf.*

citizen: a freeman or inhabitant of a town or city, an urbanite (1, *et al.*).

sport: pleasure (2).

in derision in communication: jeeringly, derisively (3).

marry: indeed, certainly (8,11).

Sir John, Master Ralph: perhaps alluding to a contemporary story in which Sir John the priest seduces Master Ralph's wife, along the lines of Heywood's *A Merry Play between John John, the husband, Tyb, his wife, and Sir John, the priest* (1533) although in Heywood's version the cuckold is called John John rather than Master Ralph (Heywood was Rastell's son-in-law); the name Ralph is typically used in sixteenth-century literature for lower-status characters; for another use of the term 'Sir John' to denote a priest, see notes to Tale 80 (9-13).

cuckold: a man with an unfaithful wife (12,16).

The moral is among those which warn that treating others with scorn and derision can sometimes backfire, *cf.* Tales 14, 53, 60, 77 and 82.

One of four tales that are unique to 'B'.

3.   Of the wife that made her husband to go sit in the arbour in the night, while her prentice lay with her in her bed.

A WIFE there was which had appointed her prentice to come to her bed in the night, which servant had long wooed her to have his pleasure. Which according to the appointment came to her bedside in the night, her
5   husband lying by her. And when she perceived him there, she caught him by the hand and held him fast, and incontinent wakened her husband and said, 'Sir, it is so:— Ye have a false and an untrue servant to you, which is William your prentice, and hath long wooed me to have
10   his pleasure, and because I could not avoid his importunate request, I have appointed him this night to meet me in the garden in the arbour. And if ye will array yourself in mine array and go thither, ye shall see the proof thereof, and then ye may rebuke him as ye think best by your discretion.'

15   This husband, thus advertised by his wife, put upon him his wife's raiment and went to the arbour. And when he was gone thither, the prentice came into bed to his mistress where for a season they were both content and pleased each other by the space of an hour or two. But when she
20   thought time convenient, she said to the prentice, 'Now go thy way into the arbour and meet him, and take a good waster in thy hand, and say thou didst it but to prove whether I would be a good woman or no, and reward him as thou thinkest best.'

This prentice, doing after his mistress' counsel, went 25
into the arbour where he found his master in his mistress'
apparel and said, 'Ah, thou harlot! Art thou come hither?
Now I see well, if I would be false to my master, thou wouldst
be a strong whore, but I had liever thou were hanged than
I would do him so traitorous a deed. Therefore I shall give 30
thee some punishment as thou like an whore hast deserved,'
and therewith lapped him well about the shoulders and
back, and gave him a dozen or two good stripes.

The master, feeling himself somewhat to smart, said,
'Peace, William, mine own true good servant! For God's 35
sake, hold thy hands, for I am thy master and not thy
mistress!'

'Nay, whore,' quod he, 'thou liest! Thou art but an harlot,
and I did but to prove thee,' and smote him again.

'Alas, man,' quod the master, 'I beseech thee, no more, 40
for I am not she, for I am thy master. Feel, for I have a beard!'

And therewith he spared his hand and felt his beard.

'Alas, master,' quod the prentice, 'I cry you mercy.'

And then the master went unto his wife and she asked
him how he had sped, and he answered, 'Iwis, wife, I have 45
been shrewdly beaten. Howbeit, I have cause to be glad, for,
I thank God, I have as true a wife and as true a servant as
any man hath in England.'

By this tale ye may see that it is not wisdom for a man to be
ruled always after his wife's counsel. 50

A.2: Of the wyfe who lay with her prentys and caused him to beate her husbande disguised in her rayment.

B.3: Of the wyfe that mayd hyr husbande to go syt in the herber in the nyght, while her prentys lay with her in her bed.

prentice: an indentured servant, an apprentice (1, *et al.*).

incontinent: straight away, immediately (7).

advertised: informed, warned (15).

raiment: clothing, apparel (16).

waster: a cudgel, a club (22).

prove: to test (22).

liever: rather (29).

lapped: gripped, embraced (32).

stripes: lashes or blows from a whip or rod, or the marks or weals left by such lashes (33).

sped: fared, done, got on (45).

iwis: certainly, indeed (45).

shrewdly: badly, dreadfully (46).

The moral is one of several concerned with the nature and status of women, *cf.* Tales 10, 11, 19, 23, 29, 35, 46, 49, 58, 66 and 97.

This tale, from Boccaccio's *Decameron* and Poggio's *Facetiae*, is a version of the medieval fabliau 'La bourgeoise d'Orléans'.

The same tale is retold in *The Sack Full of News* (1557):

There was an old man that could not well see, who had a fair young wife, and with them dwelt a young man, which had long wooed his mistress to have his pleasure of her; who at the last consented to him, but they knew not how to bring it to pass, for she did never go abroad but in her husband's company, and led him always. At last she devised a very fine shift, and bade her servant that he should that night, about midnight, come into her chamber where her husband and she lay, and she would find some device for him.

Night came, and the old man and wife went to bed, but she slept not a wink, but thought still upon her pretended purpose, but a little before the time prefixed she awakened her husband and said thus unto him, 'Sir, I will tell you a thing in secret, which your servant was purposed to do when I am alone. I can never be at quiet for him, but he is always enticing me to have me at his will, and so at the last, to be quit with him, I consented to meet him in the garden, but for mine honesty's sake I will not. Wherefore, I pray you put on my clothes and go meet him. So, when he comes to you, beat him well, and chide him, for I know well he will not strike you, because you are his master, and then he may amend himself and prove a good servant,' and the man was well pleased therewith.

So, the good man put on his wife's clothes and took a good cudgel in his hand, and went into the garden. At length, there came the servant to his mistress, where she lay in bed, and did what he would with her, and she was content. And then she told him how she had sent her husband into the garden in her apparel, and wherefore and to what purpose. So her servant arose and, as she bade him, took a good staff with him, and went into the garden as though he knew not it was his master, and said unto him, 'Nay, you whore, I did this but only to prove thee, whether thou wouldst be false to my good master, and not that I would do such a vile thing with thee!'

Whereupon, he fell upon his master giving him many sore stripes, and beating him most cruelly, still calling him nothing but, 'Out, you whore! Will you offer this abuse to my good Master?'

'Alas,' quod his Master, 'good John, I am thy master. Strike me no more I pray thee.'

'Nay, whore!' quod he, 'I know who thou art well enough.' And so he struck him again, beating him most grievously.

'Good John,' said his master, 'feel! I have a beard.'

Then the servant felt, knowing well who it was, who presently kneeled down, and cried his master mercy.

'Now, thanks be to God,' quod his master, 'I have as good a servant of thee as a man can have, and I have as good a wife as the world affords.'

Afterwards, the master went to bed and his servant also. When the old man came to bed to his wife she demanded of him how he sped. He answered and said, 'By my troth. wife, I have the trustiest servant in the world and as faithful a wife, for my servant came thither with a great staff and did beat me right sore, thinking it had been you, whereupon I was well pleased therewith.'

But ever after the servant was well beloved of his master, but better of his mistress, for his master had no mistrust of him, though he had made him a cuckold. So, the poor man was cruelly beaten, and made a summer's bird nevertheless.

4. Of him that played the Devil and came through the warren, and made them that stole the coneys to run away.

IT FORTUNED that in a market town in the county of Suffolk, there was a stage play, in the which play, one called John Adroyns, which dwelled in another village two mile from thence, played the Devil. And when the play was done, this John Adroyns in the evening departed from the said market town to go home to his own house, and because he had there no change of clothing, he went forth in his Devil's apparel. Which, in the way coming homeward, came through a warren of coneys belonging to a gentleman of the village where he himself dwelt. At which time, it fortuned a priest, a vicar of a church thereby, with two or three other unthrifty fellows, had brought with them a horse, a haye and a ferret, to the intent there to get coneys. And when the ferret was in the earth, and the haye set over the pathway where this John Adroyns should come, this priest and his other fellows saw him come in the Devil's raiment, considering that they were in the Devil's service and stealing of coneys, and supposing it had been the Devil indeed, for fear ran away.

This John Adroyns in the Devil's raiment, and because it was somewhat dark, saw not the haye, but went forth in haste and stumbled thereat and fell down, that with the fall he had almost broken his neck.

But when he was a little revived, he looked up and spied it was a haye to catch coneys, and looked further and saw that they ran away for fear of him, and saw a horse tied to a bush laden with coneys which they had taken. And he took the horse and the haye, and leaped upon the horse and rode to the gentleman's place that was lord of the warren to the intent to have thank for taking such a prey, and when he came, knocked at the gates. To whom anon, one of gentleman's servants asked who was there, and suddenly opened the gate, and as soon as he perceived him in the Devil's raiment was suddenly abashed, and sparred the door again and went in to his master, and said and swore to his master that the Devil was at the gate and would come in.

The gentleman hearing him say so, called another of his servants and bade him go to the gate to know who was there. This second servant came to the gate, durst not open it, but asked with loud voice who was there.

This John Adroyns in the Devil's apparel answered with a high voice and said, 'Tell thy master I must needs speak with him ere I go.'

This second servant hearing that answer, supposing also it had been the Devil, went in again to his master and said thus: 'Master, it is the Devil indeed that is at the gate, and saith he must needs speak with you ere he go hence.'

50 The gentleman then began a little to abash, and called the steward of his house which was the wisest servant that he had, and bade him to go to the gate and to bring him sure word who was there. This steward, because he thought he would see surely who was there, came to the

55 gate and looked through the chinks of the gate in diverse places, and saw well that it was the Devil and sat upon an horse, and hanging about the saddle on every side saw the coney heads hanging down. Then he came to his master afeard in great haste and said, 'By God's Body, it is the

60 Devil indeed that is at the gate sitting upon an horse laden all with souls, and by likelihood he is come for your soul purposely, and lacketh but your soul. And if he had your soul, I ween he should be gone.'

This gentleman then marvellously abashed, called up

65 his chaplain and made the holy candle to be lit and got holy water and went to the gate with as many of his servants as durst go with him, where the chaplain with holy words of conjuration said, 'In the name of the Father, Son and Holy Ghost, I conjure thee and charge thee in the

70 holy name of God, to tell me why and wherefore thou comest hither.'

This John Adroyns in the Devil's apparel, hearing them begin to conjure after such manner, said, 'Nay, nay, be not afeard of me, for I am a good devil! I am John Adroyns, your neighbour dwelling in this town, and he that played the Devil today in the play. I have brought my master a dozen or two of his own coneys that were stolen in his warren, and their horse and their haye, and made them for fear to run away.'

And when they heard him thus speak, by his voice they knew him well enough and opened the gate and let him come in. And so all the foresaid fear and dread was turned to mirth and disport.

By this tale ye may see that men fear many times more than they need, which hath caused men to believe that spirits and devils have been seen in diverse places, when it hath been nothing so.

A.3: *Of John Adroyns in the dyuyls apparell.*
B.4: *Of hym that playd the deuyll and came thorow the waren & mayd them that stole the connys to ronne away.*
D.2: *Of him that played, &c.*

stage play: this is probably a touring production, with local actors taking minor roles (2).

coneys: rabbits—the word 'coney' was pronounced /kʌni/ to rhyme with 'money' (10, *et al.*).

gentleman: a lord of the manor—one step down from a knight or esquire (10, *et al.*).

unthrifty: disreputable (12).

haye: a net to catch rabbits (13, *et al.*).

raiment: clothing, apparel (17, *et al.*).

anon: soon, presently, shortly (32).

suddenly: instantly, immediately (34, 35).

abashed, abash: perturbed or disconcerted, to be perturbed or disconcerted (35, *et al.*).

sparred: locked, shut, barred (36).

durst: dared (41, 67).

a high voice: a loud voice (44).

ere: before (49).

afeard: afraid (59, 74).

ween: suppose, expect, hope (63).

conjuration: invocation, exorcism (68).

conjure: to invoke, to exorcise (69, 73).

disport: amusement, fun (83).

The moral suggests we are inherently prone to mistaken supernatural fears, *cf.* Tale 18.

5. Of the sick man that bequeathed his third son a little ground with the gallows.

THERE was a rich man which lay sore sick in his bed like to die, wherefore his eldest son came to him and beseeched him to give him his blessing. To whom the father said, 'Son, thou shalt have God's blessing and mine, and because thou hast been ever good of conditions, I give and bequeath thee all my land.'

To whom he answered and said, 'Nay, father, I trust you shall live and occupy them yourself full well, by God's grace.'

Soon after, came his second son to him likewise and desired his blessing. To whom the father said, 'Because thou hast been ever kind and gentle, I give thee God's blessing and mine, and also I bequeath thee all my movable goods.'

To whom he answered and said, 'Nay, father, I trust ye shall live and do well, and spend and use your goods yourself, by God's grace.'

Anon after, the third son came to him and desired his blessing. To whom the father answered and said, 'Because thou hast been evil and stubborn of conditions and wouldst never be ruled after my counsel, I have neither land nor goods unbequeathed, but only a little vacant ground where a gallows standeth, which now I give and bequeath to thee, and God's curse withal.'

68

To whom the son answered as his brethren did and said, 25
'Nay, father, I trust ye shall live and be in good health, and
have it and occupy it yourself, by God's grace.'

But after that the father died, and this third son
continued still his unthrifty conditions, wherefore it was
his fortune afterward for his deserving to be hanged on 30
the same gallows.

*By this tale men may well perceive that young people that
will not be ruled by their friends' counsel in youth, in times
come to a shameful end.*

A.4: *Of the Ryche man and his two sonnes.*
B.5: *Of the syk man that bequethyd hys thyrd son a lyttyll ground with the galows.*
D.3: *The sick man, &c.*

gallows: a scaffold or pole where criminals are executed by hanging (23, 31).

conditions: habits, nature (5, *et al.*).

anon: soon, presently, shortly (18).

unthrifty: profligate, spendthrift (29).

for his deserving: because he deserved it (30).

The moral is among several which contrast wisdom, learning and orderly behaviour
with foolishness, wilfulness and stupidity, *cf.* Tales 1, 8, 34, 37, 67, 69, 71, 73, 75 and 81.

6.   Of the cuckold who gained a ring
by his judgement.

TWO gentlemen of acquaintance were appointed to lie with a gentlewoman in one night, the one not knowing of the other, at diverse times. This first at his hour appointed came and, in the bed there he fortuned to lose a ring. The second gentleman when he was gone, came and fortuned to find the same ring, and when he had sped his business, departed.

And two or three days after, the first gentleman seeing his ring on the other's finger challenged it of him, and he denied it him and bade him tell where he had lost it, and he said in such a gentlewoman's bed.

Then quod the other, 'And there found I it!'

And the one said he would have it, and the other said he should not. Then they agreed to be judged by the next man that they met, and it fortuned them to meet with the husband of the said gentlewoman, and desired him of his best judgement, showing him all the whole matter.

Then quod he, 'By my judgement, he that owned the sheets should have the ring.'

Then quod they, 'And for your good judgement, you shall have the ring.'

A.5: *Of the Cockolde who gained a Ring by his iudgment.*
B.6: *Of the gentylman that lost his ryng in the gentylwomans bed, & a nother gentylman
found it after in the same bed.*

of acquaintance: who knew one another (1).

appointed: resolved, decided, agreed (1, 4).

sped: done, sorted, carried out (7).

From *Cent Nouvelles Nouvelles* (1461-2) attributed to Antoine de la Salle.

A similar story is employed by Dekker and Webster in *Northward Ho!* Act I Scene i (1607).

7. Of the husbandman that asked for Master Pisspot the Physician.

IN a village in Sussex there dwelled a husbandman whose wife fortuned to fall sick. This husbandman came to the priest of the church and desired his counsel what thing was best to help his wife, which answered him and said that in Bread Street in London there was a cunning physician whose name is called Master Jordan. 'Go to him, and show him that thy wife is sick and impotent and not able to go, and show him her water and beseech him to be good master to thee, and pray him to do his cure upon her, and I warrant he will teach thee some medicine that shall help her.'

This husbandman, following his counsel, came to London and asked of diverse men which was the way to Good Ale Street, so that every man that heard him laughed him to scorn. At the last, one that heard him asked him whether it were not Bread Street that he would have.

'By God,' quod the husbandman, 'ye say truth, for I wist well it was either bread or drink!'

So when they had taught him the way to Bread Street and was entered into the street, he asked of diverse men where one Master Pisspot dwelled, which said they knew no such man and laughed at him apace. At last one asked him whether it were not Master Jordan, the physician.

'Yea, the same,' quod the husbandman, 'for I wot well a jordan and a pisspot is all one.'

So, when they had showed him his house, he went thither and came to him and did his errand thus and said, 'Sir, if it please your mastership, I understand ye are called a cunning confusion. So it is, my wife is sick and omnipotent and may not go, and here I have brought you her water. I beseech you, do your courage upon her, and I shall give your mastership a good reward.'

The physician perceiving by the water that she was weak of nature, bade him get her meat that were restorative, and specially if he could let her have a poundgarnet, and to let her not overcome her stomach with much meat till she have an appetite.

This husbandman heard him speak of a poundgarnet and an appetite, had weened he had spoken of a pound of garlic and of an ape, and shortly bought a pound of garlic and after went to the Steelyard and bought an ape of one of the merchants, and brought both home to his wife, and tied the ape with a chain at his bed's foot, and made his wife to eat the pound of garlic whether she would or no. Whereby, she fell in so great a lask that it purged all the corruption out of her body; whereby, and by reason that the ape that was tied there made so many mocks, skips and knacks that made her oft times to be merry and laugh that, thanked be God, she was shortly restored to health.

By this tale ye may see that oft times medicines taken at adventures do as much good to the patient as medicines given by the solemn counsel of cunning physicians.

husbandman: a tenant farmer or smallholder (1, *et al.*).

Bread Street: this street runs south from Cheapside to the old bank of the Thames (5, *et al.*).

cunning: skilful, knowledgable (6, *et al.*).

impotent: incapable, powerless (7).

her water: her urine (8, 31).

Good Ale Street: the husbandman has confused bread and ale, twin staples of his diet (14).

wist, wot: knew, know (16, 24).

I wot well a jordan and a pisspot is all one: a 'jordan' was a colloquial term for a chamber pot, presumably because it was supposed to flow like the River Jordan (24-5).

a cunning confusion: the husbandman has confused 'physician' with 'confusion' (29).

omnipotent: the husbandman has confused 'impotent' meaning 'powerless', with 'omnipotent' meaning 'all powerful' (30).

do your courage: the husbandman has confused 'cure' with 'courage'; in this context, the word 'courage' could suggest 'will, desire, lust' (31).

weak of nature: this phrase could suggest a range of meanings, but here indicates that she is suffering from constipation (34).

meat: food (34).

poundgarnet: a pomegranate (36, 38).

weened: thought (39).

shortly: promptly, quickly (40, 49).

Steelyard: the merchants of the Hanseatic League were based at the Steelyard, just west of London Bridge, from the thirteenth century onwards; the site is where Cannon Street Station stands today (41).

lask: flux, diarrhoea (45).

knacks: sharp noises such as clicks, knocks and cracks (48).

at adventures: by chance (50-1).

One of four tales that are unique to 'B'.

8. Of the scholar that bore his shoes to clouting.

IN the University of Oxford there was a scholar that delighted much to speak eloquent English and curious terms, and came to the cobbler with his shoes, which were picked before as they used that season, to have them clouted, and said this wise:

'Cobbler, I pray thee set me two triangles and two semicircles upon my subpeditals, and I shall give thee for thy labour.'

The cobbler, because he understood him not half well, answered shortly and said, 'Sir, your eloquence passeth mine intelligence, but I promise you, if ye meddle with me, the clouting of your shoon shall cost you three pence.'

By this tale men may learn that it is folly to study to speak eloquently before them that be rude and unlearned.

A.6: *Of the scoler that gave his shoes to cloute.*
B.8: *Of the scoler that bare his shoys to cloutyng.*
D.4: *The scholer that bare his &c.*

clouting: patching; in this case, patching the worn soles of shoes with 'clump soles' (12).

curious: abstruse, sophisticated (2).

picked before: 'pointed in front'; the pointy-toed Crakow or Poulaine shoe had been fashionable during the fifteenth century—their fall from fashion coincided with the accession of King Henry VII, and by Rastell's day they had been ousted by the broad-toed 'cow-mouth' or 'duckbill' shoes seen in the paintings of Holbein (4).

clouted: patched (5).

subpeditals: soles—although the words 'triangle' and 'semicircle' are familiar enough for modern readers, these mathematical terms were almost as alien to everyday sixteenth-century English as the word 'subpedital' for 'shoe sole', and would have seemed equally out-of-place in a cobbler's workshop (7).

shortly: briskly, hastily (10).

meddle with: to have dealings with, to be concerned with (11).

shoon: shoes (12).

three pence: the equivalent of about £6.50 today (12).

rude: uneducated, uncouth (14).

The moral is among several which contrast wisdom, learning and orderly behaviour with foolishness, wilfulness and stupidity, cf. Tales 1, 5, 34, 37, 67, 69, 71, 73, 75 and 81.

9. Of him that said that a woman's tongue was lightest meat of digestion.

A CERTAIN artificer in London there was, which was sore sick, that could not well digest his meat, to whom a physician came to give him counsel, and said that he must use to eat meats that be light of digestion, as small birds, as sparrows or swallows, and specially that bird that is called a wagtail whose flesh is marvellous light of digestion because that bird is ever moving and stirring.

The sick man, hearing the physician say so, answered him and said, 'Sir, if that be the cause that those birds be light of digestion, then I know a meat much lighter of digestion than either sparrow, swallow or wagtail, and that is my wife's tongue, for it is never in rest but ever moving and stirring.'

By this tale ye may learn a good general rule of physic.

A.7: *Of him that said that a womans tongue was lightest of digestion.*
B.9: *Of hym that sayd that a womans tong was lightist met of degestion.*
D.5: *A womans tong, &c.*

artificer: a craftsman, an artisan (1).

light of digestion: easy to digest (4, *et al.*).

physic: medicine (14).

The moral here may be intended as ironic, *cf.* Tales 7 and 39.

From *Summa Praedicantium* by John of Bromyard (d.1352) and Heinrich Bebel's *Facetiae* (1506).

Rastell makes use of the same joke in a passage of his *Interlude of the Four Elements* (c.1519):
     HUMANITY: Thou art a mad guest, by this light!
     SENSUAL APPETITE: Yea, Sir, it is a fellow that never fails—
       But canst get my master a dish of quails,
       Small birds, swallows, or wagtails?
       They be light of digestion.
     TAVERNER: Light of digestion? For what reason?
     SEN: For physic putteth this reason thereto,
       Because those birds fly to and fro,
       And be continual moving.
     TAV: Then know I of a lighter meat than that.
     HUM: I pray thee, tell me what.
     TAV: If ye will needs know at short and long,
       It is even a woman's tongue,
       For that is ever stirring.

10. Of the woman that followed her fourth husband's hearse and wept.

A WOMAN there was which had had four husbands. It fortuned also that this fourth husband died and was brought to church upon the bier, whom this woman followed and made great moan and waxed very sorry,
5 insomuch that her neighbours thought she would swoon and die for sorrow. Wherefore, one of her gossips came to her and spoke to her in her ear, and bade her for God's sake comfort herself and refrain that lamentation, or else it would hurt her greatly and peradventure put
10 her in jeopardy of her life.

To whom this woman answered and said, 'Iwis, good gossip, I have great cause to mourn if ye knew all, for I have buried three husbands beside this man, but I was never in the case that I am now, for there was not one of
15 them but when that I followed the corpse to church, yet I was sure of another husband before the corpse came out of my house, and now I am sure of none other husband, and therefore ye may be sure I have great cause to be sad and heavy.'

20 *By this tale ye may see that the old proverb is true, that it is as great pity to see a woman weep as a goose to go barefoot.*

A.8: *Of the Woman that followed her fourth husbands bere and wept.*
B.10: *Of the woman that followyd her fourth husbandys herce & wept.*
D.6: *Of the woman that had, &c.*

waxed: grew, became (4).

sorry: sad, sorrowful (4).

gossip: a godparent or godchild, a close friend or companion (6,12).

peradventure: perhaps (9).

iwis: certainly, indeed (11).

as great pity ... go barefoot: this proverb is also found among other places in Bale's *King Johan* (1538), Burton's *Anatomy of Melancholy* (1621) and it is listed in Ray's *Proverbs* (1670); a close variant appears in Puttenham's *Art of English Poesy* (1589) (20-1).

The moral is one of several concerned with the nature and status of women, *cf.* Tales 3, 11, 19, 23, 29, 35, 46, 49, 58, 66 and 97.

11. Of the woman that said her wooer came too late.

ANOTHER woman there was that kneeled at the Mass of Requiem, while the corpse of her husband lay on the bier in the church. To whom a young man came and spoke with her in her ear, as though it had been for some matter concerning the funerals. Howbeit, he spoke of no such matter, but only wooed her that he might be her husband. To whom she answered and said thus:

'Sir, by my troth, I am sorry that ye come so late, for I am sped already, for I was made sure yesterday to another man.'

By this tale ye may perceive that women oft times be wise and loath to lose any time.

A.9: *Of the Woman that sayd her woer came to late.*
B.11: *Of the woman that sayd her wooer came too late.*
D.7: *The woman that said hir, &c.*

Mass of Requiem: the funeral service (1-2).

funerals: funeral rites, obsequies; invariably a plural in earlier forms of English (5).

sped: fixed up, sorted, having achieved one's goal (9).

made sure: betrothed, promised in marriage (9).

The moral is one of several concerned with the nature and status of women, *cf.* Tales 3, 10, 19, 23, 29, 35, 46, 49, 58, 66 and 97.

From Heinrich Bebel's *Facetiae* (1506).

12. Of the miller with the golden thumb.

A MERCHANT that thought to deride a miller, said
unto the miller sitting among company, 'Sir, I have
heard say that every true miller that tolleth truly hath a
golden thumb.'

5   The miller answered and said it was true.

Then quod the merchant, 'I pray thee let me see thy
thumb.'

And when the miller showed his thumb, the merchant
said, 'I cannot perceive that thy thumb is gilt, but it is as
10   all other men's thumbs be.'

To whom the miller answered and said, 'Sir, truth it is
that my thumb is gilt. Howbeit, ye have no power to see it,
for there is a property ever incident thereto, that he that
is a cuckold shall never have power to see it.'

A.10: *Of the Mylner with the golden thombe.*
B.12: *Of the mylner with the golden thombe.*
D.8: *Of a marchant & ane miller.*

every true miller ... golden thumb: this proverb is also alluded to in Chaucer's *Canterbury Tales* (c.1400), *Cock Lorrell's Boat* (c.1510), Gascoigne's *Steel Glass* (1562), and elsewhere (3-4).

tolleth: assesses a rate or fee (3).

cuckold: a man with an unfaithful wife (14).

13. Of the horseman of Ireland that prayed O'Conor to hang up the friar.

ONE which was called O'Conor, an Irish lord, took an horseman prisoner that was one of his great enemies. Which, for any request or entreaty that the horseman made, gave judgement that he should incontinent be hanged, and made a friar to shrive him and bade him make him ready to die.

This friar that shrove him examined him of diverse sins and asked him among other, which were the greatest sins that ever he did. This horseman answered and said, 'One of the greatest acts that ever I did which I now most repent, is that when I took O'Conor the last week in a church, and there I might have burned him, church and all, and because I had conscience and pity of burning of the church, I tarried the time so long that O'Conor escaped. And that same deferring of burning of the church and so long tarrying of that time is one of the worst acts that ever I did, whereof I most repent.'

This friar perceiving him in that mind said, 'Peace man, in the name of God, and change thy mind and die in Charity, or else thou shalt never come in Heaven.'

'Nay,' quod the horseman, 'I will never change that mind, whatsoever shall come to my soul!'

This friar perceiving him thus still to continue his mind, came to O'Conor and said, 'Sir, in the name of God, have some pity upon this man's soul, and let him not die now till he be in a better mind. For if he die now, he is so far out of Charity that utterly his soul shall be damned,' and showed him what mind he was in, and all the whole matter as is before showed.

This horseman hearing the friar thus entreat for him, said to O'Conor thus:

'O'Conor, thou seest well by this man's report that, if I die now, I am out of Charity and not ready to go to Heaven, and so it is that I am now out of Charity indeed. But thou seest well, that this friar is a good man. He is now well disposed and in Charity, and he is ready to go to Heaven, and so am not I. Therefore I pray thee, hang up this friar while that he his ready to go to Heaven, and let me tarry till another time, that I may be in Charity and ready and meet to go to Heaven.'

This O'Conor hearing this mad answer of him, spared the man and forgave him his life at that season.

By this ye may see that he that is in danger of his enemy that hath no pity, he can do no better than show to him the uttermost of his malicious mind which that he beareth toward him.

A.11: *Of the horseman of Irelande that prayde Oconer for to hange up the frere.*
B.13: *Of the horsman of yrelond that prayd Oconer to hang vp the frere.*

O'Conor: the royal family of Connacht had been O'Conors until the death of Felim O'Conor, King of Connacht, in 1474 (1, *et al.*).

incontinent: straight away, immediately (4).

shrive: to hear Confession, to grant Absolution of sins through Confession (5).

Charity: love, the love of God (20, *et al.*).

meet: fit, befitted (40).

mad: wild, irrational, harebrained (41).

The moral may be compared with that for Tale 61.

14. Of the priest that said neither 'Corpus meus' nor 'Corpum meum.'

THE Archdeacon of Essex that had been long in authority, in a time of Visitation when all the priests appeared before him, called aside three of the young priests which were accused that they could not well say their Divine Service, and asked of them, when they said Mass whether they said 'Corpus meus' or 'Corpum meum.'

The first priest said that he said 'Corpus meus.'

The second said that he said 'Corpum meum.'

And then he asked of the third how he said, which answered and said thus:

'Sir, because it is so great a doubt, and diverse men be in diverse opinions, therefore because I would be sure I would not offend, when I come to the place, I leave it clean out and say nothing therefore.'

Wherefore the archdeacon then openly rebuked them all three. But diverse that were present thought more default in him, because he himself beforetime had admitted them to be priests.

By this tale ye may see that one ought to take heed how he rebuketh another, lest it turn most to his own rebuke.

A.12: *Of the preest that sayd nother Corpus meus nor Corpum meum.*
B.14: *Of the prest that sayd nother corpus meus nor corpum meum.*
D.10: *The Preist that said, &c.*

Corpus meus, Corpum meum: the phrase, *Hoc est corpus meum* 'This is my body' appears in the Latin of the Vulgate New Testament (Matthew 26:26, Mark 14:22, Luke 22:19, 1 Corinthians 11:24) and is the cornerstone of the Mass, as it is the moment when the bread becomes the Flesh of God; this Latin phrase (correctly *'corpus meum'*) thus underpins the central mystery of medieval Christian spirituality (6, *et al.*).

archdeacon: the bishop's official responsible for churches and marriages; the Archdeaconry of Essex was within the Diocese of London, and from 1503, the position was held by Richard Rawson (d.1543) chaplain to King Henry VIII (1, 15).

Visitation: inspection by an ecclesiastical superior (2).

Divine Service: the Mass (5).

default: fault (17).

beforetime: earlier (17).

The moral is among those which warn that treating others with scorn and derision can sometimes backfire, *cf.* Tales 2, 53, 60, 77 and 82.

15. Of the two friars, whereof the one loved not the eel head nor the other the tail.

TWO friars sat at a gentleman's table, which had before him on a fasting day an eel, and cut the head off the eel and laid it upon one of the friars' trenchers. But the friar, because he would have had of the middle part of the eel, said to the gentleman he loved no eel heads.

This gentleman also cut the tail off the eel and laid it on the other friar's trencher. He likewise, because he would have had of the middle part of the eel, said he loved no eel tails.

This gentleman perceiving that, gave the tail to him that said he loved not the head, and gave the head to him that said he loved not the tail. And as for the middle part of the eel, he ate part himself and part he gave to other folk at the table. Wherefore, these friars for anger would eat never a morsel, and so they, for all their craft and subtlety, were not only deceived of the best morsel of the eel, but thereof had no part at all.

By this ye see that they that covet the best part sometime therefore lose the mean part and all.

A.13: *Of the two freres whereof the one loued nat the ele heed nor the other the tayle.*
B.15: *Of the .ii. frerys wherof the one louyd not the eel head nor the other the tayle.*
D.11: *Of two freirs the one loued &c.*

fasting day: much of the medieval Christian year was given over to fast days, when it was forbidden to eat animal foodstuffs such as meat, eggs or dairy products, which were replaced with fish or beans (2).

trencher: a plate, a dish (3, 7).

craft: cleverness, ingenuity, craftiness (15).

subtlety: cunning, craftiness (15).

mean: common, shared, inferior (19).

The moral is one of several concerned with covetousness, miserliness, and attitudes to money and personal possessions, *cf.* Tales 17, 20, 33, 62, 68, 78, 90, 91 and 100.

16.   Of the Welshman that shrove him for breaking his fast on the Friday.

A WELSHMAN dwelling in a wild place of Wales came to his curate in the time of Lent and was confessed. And when his confession was in manner at the end, the curate asked him whether he had any other thing to say that grieved his conscience. Which, sore abashed, answered no word a great while. At last, by exhortation of his ghostly father, he said that there was one thing in his mind that greatly grieved his conscience, which he was ashamed to utter for it was so grievous that he trowed God would never forgive him.

To whom the curate answered and said that God's mercy was above all, and bade him not despair in the mercy of God for, whatsoever it was, if he were repentant, that God would forgive him. And so by long exhortation, at the last he showed it, and said thus:

'Sir, it happened once that, as my wife was making a cheese upon a Friday, I would fain have sayed whether it had been salt or fresh, and took a little of the whey in my hand and put it in my mouth, and ere I was ware, part of it went down my throat against my will, and so I broke my fast.'

To whom the curate said, 'And if there be none other thing, I warrant God shall forgive thee.'

So, when he had well comforted him with the mercy of God, the curate prayed him to answer a question and to tell him truth. And when the Welshman had promised to tell the truth, the curate said that there were robberies and murders done nigh the place where he dwelt, and diverse men found slain, and asked him whether he were consenting to any of them. To whom he answered and said, 'Yes,' and said he was party to many of them, and did help to rob and to slay diverse of them.

Then the curate asked him why he did not confess him thereof. The Welshman answered and said he took that for no sin, for it was a custom among them that when any booty came of any rich merchant riding, that it was but a good neighbour's deed one to help another when one called another, and so they took that but for good fellowship and neighbourhood.

Here may ye see that some have remorse of conscience of small venial sins, and fear not to do great offences without shame of the world or dread of God, and as the common proverb is, 'they stumble at a straw, and leap over a block.'

A.14: *Of the welche man that shroue hym for brekynge of hys faste on the fryday.*
B.16: *Of the welchman that shroue hym for brekyng his fast on the fryday.*

shrove: confessed.

curate: a priest charged with the cure or care of souls, a parish priest (2, *et al.*).

in manner: after a fashion, so to speak, more or less (3).

abashed: perturbed, disconcerted (6).

ghostly: spiritual (7).

trowed: believed (10).

cheese: regarded as the Welsh national dish—see for example, Shakespeare's *Merry Wives*, Act V, scene v (17).

fain: gladly, wishfully, heartily (17).

sayed: assayed, tested, judged (17).

salt or fresh: salted cheese could be ripened and kept for the winter, while unsalted cheese was eaten fresh (18).

whey: milk is separated into solid curds and liquid whey, so that cheese can be made from the curds (18).

ere: before (19).

ware: aware (19).

venial sins: ordinary or less serious sins (42).

stumble at a straw ... block: this proverb is quoted by Palsgrave in *L'esclarcissement de la langue francoyse* (1530); it is alluded to in Tyndale's *The Obedience of a Christian Man* (1528) and Spenser's *The Shepherds' Calendar* (1579), and is the subject of two epigrams by John Heywood (1562) (44).

From Poggio's *Facetiae*, where the aspersions cast here upon the Welsh are thrown instead on the Neapolitans.

17. Of the merchant of London that put nobles in his mouth in his deathbed.

ARICH covetous merchant there was that dwelled in London, which ever gathered money and could never find in his heart to spend aught upon himself nor upon no man else. Which fell sore sick, and as he lay on his deathbed, had his purse lying at his bed's head, and had such a love to his money that he put his hand in his purse and took out thereof ten or twelve pounds in nobles, and put them in his mouth. And because his wife and other perceived him very sick and like to die, they exhorted him to be confessed and brought the curate unto him. Which, when they had caused him to say 'Benedicite,' the curate bade him cry God mercy and show to Him his sins.

Then this sick man began to say, 'I cry God mercy, I have offended in the Seven Deadly Sins and broken the Ten Commandments.' And because of the gold in his mouth he muffled so in his speech that the curate could not well understand him, wherefore the curate asked him what he had in his mouth that letted his speech.

'Iwis, Master Parson,' quod the sick man muffling, 'I have nothing in my mouth but a little money. Because I wot not whither I shall go, I thought I would take some spending money with me, for I wot not what need I shall have thereof,' and incontinent after that saying, died before he was confessed or repentant that any man could perceive, and so by likelihood went to the Devil. 25

By this tale ye may see that they that all their lives will never do charity to their neighbours, that God in time of their death will not suffer them to have grace of repentance.

A.15: *Of the merchaunte of London that dyd put nobles in his mouthe in hys dethe bedde.*
B.17: *Of the merchaunt of london that put nobles in his mouth in his deth bed.*

noble: a gold coin usually valued at 6s. 8d. (the equivalent of about £175 today) but which, for much of the previous century, had been worth more on foreign markets, making it particularly highly prized by merchants (8).

ten or twelve pounds: the equivalent of about £5,200 to £6,250 today (7).

curate: a priest charged with the cure or care of souls, a parish priest (10, *et al.*).

Benedicite: 'Bless me,' words spoken by the penitent as the preliminary to Confession (12).

Seven Deadly Sins, Ten Commandments: see Tale 57 'Of the friar that preached the Ten Commandments' (15-6).

muffled: covered his face or mouth—here suggesting muffled speech (17).

letted: hindered, impeded (19).

iwis: certainly, indeed (20).

muffling: covering his mouth (20).

wot: know (23).

incontinent: straight away, immediately (24).

The moral is one of several concerned with covetousness, miserliness, and attitudes to money and personal possessions, *cf.* Tales 15, 20, 33, 62, 68, 78, 90, 91 and 100.

18.   Of the miller that stole the nuts and of the tailor that stole a sheep.

THERE was a certain rich husbandman in a village which loved nuts marvellously well, and set trees of filberts and other nut trees in his orchard, and nourished them well all his life. And when he died, he made his executors to make promise to bury with him in his grave a bag of nuts, or else they should not be his executors. Which executors, for fear of losing their rooms, fulfilled his will and did so.

It happened that the same night after that he was buried, there was a miller in a white coat came to this man's garden to the intent to steal a bag of nuts, and in the way he met with a tailor in a black coat, an unthrift of his acquaintance, and showed him his intent. This tailor likewise showed him that he intended the same time to steal a sheep, and so they both there agreed to go forward every man severally with his purpose, and after that they appointed to make good cheer each with other and to meet again in the church porch, and he that came first to tarry for the other.

This miller, when he had speed of his nuts, came first to the church porch and there tarried for his fellow, and the meanwhile, sat still there and knacked nuts.

It fortuned then the sexton of the church, because it was about nine of the clock, came to ring curfew. And when he looked in the porch and saw one all in white knacking nuts, he had weened it had been the dead man risen out of his grave knacking the nuts that were buried with him, and ran home again in all haste, and told to a cripple that was in his house what he had seen. This cripple thus hearing him, rebuked the sexton and said that if he were able to go, he would go thither and conjure the spirit. 30

'By my troth,' quod the sexton, 'and if thou durst do that, I will bear thee on my neck!' and so they both agreed.

The sexton took the cripple on his neck and came into the churchyard again, and the miller in the porch saw one 35 coming bearing a thing on his back, had weened it had been the tailor coming with the sheep, and rose up to meet them. And as he came toward them, he asked and said, 'Is he fat? Is he fat?'

The sexton, hearing him say so, for fear cast the cripple 40 down and said, 'Fat or lean, take him as he is!' and ran away. And the cripple by miracle was made whole, and ran away as fast as he or faster.

This miller, perceiving that they were two and that one ran after another, thought that one had spied the tailor 45 stealing the sheep, and that he had run after him to have taken him. And fearing that somebody also had spied him stealing the nuts, he for fear left his nuts behind him and, as secretly as he could, ran home to his mill.

50 And anon, after that he was gone, the tailor came with the stolen sheep upon his neck to the church porch to seek the miller, and when he found there the nutshells, he supposed that his fellow had been there and gone home, as he was indeed. Wherefore, he took up the sheep again
55 on his neck and went toward the mill. But yet during this while, the sexton which ran away went not to his own house but went to the parish priest's chamber, and showed him how the spirit of the man was risen out of his grave knacking nuts, as ye have heard before. Wherefore, the
60 priest said that he would go conjure him, if the sexton would go with him, and so they both agreed. The priest did on his surplice and a stole about his neck, and took holy water with him, and came with the sexton toward the church. And as soon as he entered into the churchyard,
65 the tailor with the white sheep on his neck (intending, as I before have showed you, to go down to the mill) met with them, and had weened that the priest in his surplice had been the miller in his white coat, and said to him, 'By God, I have him! I have him!' meaning thereby the sheep that
70 he had stolen.

The priest, perceiving the tailor all in black and a white thing on his neck, had weened it had been the Devil bearing away the spirit of the dead man that was buried,

and ran away as fast as he could, taking the way down
toward the mill, and the sexton running after him. 75

This tailor, seeing one following him, had weened
that one had followed the miller to have done him some
hurt, and thought he would follow if need were to help
the miller, and went forth till he came to the mill and
knocked at the mill door. The miller being within asked 80
who was there.

The tailor answered and said, 'By God, I have caught one
of them and made him sure and tied him fast by the legs!'
meaning by the sheep that he had stolen and had then on
his neck tied fast by the legs. But the miller, hearing him 85
say that he had him tied fast by the legs, had weened it had
been the constable that had taken the tailor for stealing of
the sheep and had tied him by the legs, and feared that he
had come to have taken him also for stealing of the nuts.

Wherefore the miller opened a back door, and ran 90
away as fast as he could. The tailor, hearing the back
door opening, went on the other side of the mill and
there saw the miller running away, and stood there a
little while musing, with the sheep on his neck.

Then was the parish priest and the sexton standing 95
there under the mill-house, hiding them for fear, and saw
the tailor again with the sheep on his neck, had weened
still it had been the Devil with the spirit of the dead man
on his neck, and for fear ran away. But because they knew

100 not the ground well, the priest leapt into a ditch almost
over the head like to be drowned, that he cried with a loud
voice, 'Help, help!'

Then the tailor looked about and saw the miller run
away and the sexton another way, and heard the priest cry
105 'Help,' had weened it had been the constable with a great
company crying for help to take him and to bring him to
prison for stealing of the sheep, wherefore he threw down
the sheep and ran away another way as fast as he could.

And so every man was afeared of other without cause.

110 *By this ye may see well it is folly for any man to fear a thing
too much till that he see some proof or cause.*

A.16: *Of the mylner that stale the nuttes of the tayler that stale a shepe.*
B.18: *Of the mylner that stale the nuttys & of the tayler that stale a shepe.*

husbandman: a tenant farmer or smallholder (1).

filbert: a variety of hazelnut (3).

bury with him: Christian practice has traditionally forbidden the use of grave goods, and this infringement against taboo sets the scene for the supposedly supernatural happenings which follow (5).

rooms: places, positions (7).

unthrift: a good-for-nothing (12).

appointed: resolved, decided, agreed (17).

speed: luck, fortune, prosperity, fulfilment (20).

knack: to crack a nut (22, *et al.*).

sexton: the person who looks after the church and churchyard (23, *et al.*).

weened: supposed, imagined (26, *et al.*).

conjure: to invoke, to exorcise (31, 60).

durst: dared (32).

anon: soon, presently, shortly (50).

did on: put on (62).

sure: secure (83).

constable: a law enforcement officer (87, 105).

The moral suggests we are inherently prone to mistaken supernatural fears, *cf.* Tale 4.

Oesterley suggests a connection with the thirteenth-century fabliau *Estula*, while Brewer (p.xxxi) finds parallels in *Summa Praedicantium* by John of Bromyard (d.1352), *Scala Coeli* by Johannes Gobius the Younger (d.1350), and *Alphabetum Narrationum* by Arnold of Liége (d. c.1308). None of these, however, appears to be a direct source for the tale here.

19. Of the Four Elements, where they should soon be found.

I N the old world when all thing could speak, the Four Elements met together for many things which they had to do because they must meddle alway one with another, and had communication together of diverse matters. And because they could not conclude all their matters at that season, they appointed to break communication for that time, and to meet again another time. Therefore, each one of them showed to other where their most abiding was, and where their fellows should find them if need should require.

And first the Earth said, 'Brethren, ye know well as for me, I am permanent alway and not removable, therefore ye may be sure to have me alway when ye list.'

The Water said, 'If ye list to seek me, ye shall be sure ever for to have me under a tuft of green rushes, or else in a woman's eye.'

The Wind said, 'If ye list to speak with me, ye shall be sure to have me among aspen leaves, or else in a woman's tongue.'

Then quod the Fire, 'If any of you list to seek me, ye shall ever be sure to find me in a flint stone, or else in a woman's heart.'

By this tale ye may learn as well the properties of the Four Elements as the properties of a woman.

A.17: *Of the foure elementes where they should sone be founde.*
B.19: *Of the .iiii. elementys where they shulde sone be found.*
D.12: *Of the four Elements.*

Four Elements: according to Classical Greek tradition, all matter was composed of the Four Elements of Earth, Water, Wind and Fire, a concept which underlay medieval thinking on astrology and medicine.

when all thing could speak: according to both Classical and Hebrew traditions there was a time in the beginning when animals could speak and, according to the fables Babrius, the power of speech also extended to leaves and stones (1).

meddle ... with: to have dealings with, to be concerned with (3).

appointed: resolved, decided, agreed (6).

most abiding: usual dwelling (8).

list: to please or be pleased, to wish, to choose (13, *et al.*).

aspen leaves: aspen leaves quiver or tremble in the breeze with a distinctive whispering sound—*cf.* Tale 62 'Of the man that had the dumb wife' (18).

The moral is one of several concerned with the nature and status of women, *cf.* Tales 3, 10, 11, 23, 29, 35, 46, 49, 58, 66 and 97.

Rastell's *A New Interlude and a Merry of the Nature of the Four Elements* was published in 1519.

20.   Of the woman that poured the potage in the judge's mail.

THERE was a justice but late in the realm of England called Master Vavasour, a very homely man and rude of conditions, and loved never to spend much money. This Master Vavasour rode on a time in his circuit in a
5   place of the north country, where he had agreed with the sheriff for a certain sum of money for his charges through the shire, so that at every inn and lodging this Master Vavasour paid for his own costs.

It fortuned so that when he came to a certain lodging,
10   he commanded one Turpin, his servant, to see that he used good husbandry, and to save such things as were left, and to carry it with him to serve him at the next baiting. This Turpin, doing his master's commandment, took the broken bread, broken meat and all such thing that was
15   left, and put it in his mail.

The wife of the house, perceiving that he took all such fragments and victual with him that was left and put it in his mail, she brought up the potage that was left in the pot and, when Turpin had turned his back a little aside, she
20   poured the potage into the mail, which ran upon his robe of scarlet and other of his garments, and rayed them very evil that they were much hurt therewith.

This Turpin suddenly turned him and saw it, reviled the wife therefore, and ran to his master and told him what she had done. Wherefore Master Vavasour incontinent 25 called the wife and said to her thus: 'Thou drab!' quod he. 'What hast thou done? Why hast thou poured the potage in my mail and marred my raiment and gear?'

'Oh, sir,' quod the wife, 'I know well ye are a judge of the realm, and I perceive by you, your mind is to do right and 30 to have that that is your own, and your mind is to have all thing with you that ye have paid for, both broken bread, meat and other things that is left, and so it is reason that ye have. And therefore, because your servant hath taken the bread and the meat and put it in your mail, I have 35 therefore put in your mail the potage that be left, because ye have well and truly paid for them. For if I should keep anything from you that ye have paid for, peradventure ye would trouble me in the law another time.'

Here ye may see that he that playeth the niggard too much, 40 *sometime it turneth him to his own loss.*

A.18: *Of the woman that poured the potage in the iudges male.*
B.20: *Of the woman that powryd the potage in the Juggys male.*

mail: a kind of bag; the first edition ('A') reads 'cloth sack' for 'mail' throughout, except in the title (15, *et al.*).

homely: plain, plain-spoken, blunt (2).

rude: plain, austere, unsophisticated, rough-and-ready (2).

of conditions: in his habits or ways, by nature (3).

good husbandry: economy, thrift (11).

baiting: refreshment, stopping for food (12).

potage: stew, thick soup—treated as a plural (18, *et al.*).

scarlet: an expensive woollen cloth (21).

rayed: berayed, dirtied, defiled (21).

suddenly: abruptly, unexpectedly (23).

incontinent: straight away, immediately (25).

drab: harlot, slut (26).

my raiment and gear: Turpin may be dressed in his master's livery, but it is emblematic of Vavasour's miserliness that he still considers Turpin's clothes as his own (28).

peradventure: perhaps (38).

niggard: miser (*cg.* ON *nigla*, to niggle, to fuss over little things) (40).

The moral is one of several concerned with covetousness, miserliness, and attitudes to money and personal possessions, *cf.* Tales 15, 17, 33, 62, 68, 78, 90, 91 and 100.

Hazlitt identified the protagonist here as John Vavasour, Recorder of York, who was made a justice of Common Pleas in August 1490.

Another story of Vavasour and Turpin appears in *Tales and Quick Answers* (c.1532-5):

Master Vavasour, sometime a judge of England, had a servant with him called Turpin, which had done him service many years, wherefore he came unto his master on a time, and said to him on this wise: 'Sir, I have done you service long, wherefore I pray you give me somewhat to help me in mine old age.'

'Turpin,' quod he, 'thou sayest truth, and hereon I have thought many a time. I will tell thee what thou shalt do. Now shortly I must ride up to London, and, if thou wilt bear my costs thither, I will surely give thee such a thing that shall be worth to thee an hundred pound.'

'I am content,' quod Turpin.

So all the way as he rode Turpin paid his costs, till they came to their last lodging, and there after supper he came to his master and said, 'Sir, I have borne your costs hitherto as ye bade me. Now I pray you, let me see what thing it is that should be worth an hundred pound to me.'

'Did I promise thee such a thing?' quod his master.

'Yea, forsooth,' quod Turpin.

'Show me thy writing,' quod master Vavasour.

'I have none,' said Turpin.

'Then thou art like to have nothing,' said his master. 'And learn this at me: When so ever thou makest a bargain with a man, look that thou take sure writing, and be well ware how thou makest a writing to any man. This point hath vailed me an hundred pound in my days, and so it may thee.'

When Turpin saw there was none other remedy, he held himself content. On the morrow, Turpin tarried a little behind his master to reckon with the hostess where they lay, and of her he borrowed so much money on his master's scarlet cloak as drew to all the costs that they spent by the way. Master Vavasour had not ridden past two mile but that it began to rain, wherefore he called for his cloak. His other servants said, 'Turpin was behind, and had it with him.' So they hovered under a tree till Turpin overtook them. When he was come, Master Vavasour all angrily said, 'Thou knave, why comest thou not away with my cloak?'

'Sir, and please you,' quod Turpin, 'I have laid it to gage for your costs all the way.'

'Why, knave,' quod his master, 'didst thou not promise to bear my charges to London?'

'Did I?' quod Turpin.

'Yea,' quod his master, 'that thou didst!'

'Let see, show me your writing thereof,' quod Turpin.

Whereto his master, I think, answered but little.

21. Of the wedded men that came to Heaven to claim their heritage.

A CERTAIN wedded man there was which, when he was dead, came to Heaven Gates to St Peter, and said he came to claim his heritage, which he had deserved. St Peter asked him what he was, and he said, 'A wedded man.'

5 Anon, St Peter opened the gates and bade him come in, and said he was worthy to have his heritage because he had had much trouble, and was worthy to have a Crown of Glory.

Anon after that, there came another man that claimed Heaven, and said to St Peter he had had two wives, to 10 whom St Peter answered and said, 'Come in, for thou art worthy to have a double Crown of Glory, for thou hast had double trouble.'

At the last, there came the third claiming Heaven, and said to St Peter that he had had three wives, and desired 15 to come in.

'What!' quod St Peter. 'Thou hast been once in trouble and thereof delivered, and then willingly wouldst be troubled again, and yet again thereof delivered and, for all that, couldst not beware the third time but enterest willingly 20 in trouble again! Therefore go thy way to Hell, for thou shalt never come in Heaven, for thou art not worthy.'

This tale is a warning to them that have been twice in peril to beware how they come therein the third time.

A.19: *Of the wedded men that came to heuen to clayme theyr herytage.*
B.21: *Of the weddyd men that cam to heuyn to clayme theyr herytage.*
D.13: *A weddit man yat come, &c.*

anon: soon, presently, shortly (5, 8).

Crown of Glory: one of the Five Heavenly Crowns referred to in the New Testament; according to 1 Peter 5:4, a Crown of Glory is awarded to the elders who care for the flock of God (7, 11).

22. Of the merchant that charged his son to find one to sing for his soul.

A RICH merchant of London there was, which had but one son that was somewhat unthrifty. Therefore his father upon his deathbed called him to him and said he knew well that he had been unthrifty, howbeit if he knew he would amend his conditions, he would make him his executor and leave him his goods, so that he would promise him to pray for his soul, and to find one daily to sing for him. Which thing to perform, his son there made a faithful promise.

After that, this man made him his executor and died. But after that, his son kept such riot that in short time he had wasted and spent all, and had nothing left but a hen and a cock that was his father's.

It fortuned then that one of his friends came to him and said he was sorry that he had wasted so much, and asked him how he would perform his promise made to his father that he would keep one to sing for him.

This young man answered and said, 'By God, yet I will perform my promise, for I will keep this same cock alive still, and he will crow every day, and so he shall sing every day for my father's soul, and so I will perform my promise well enough.'

By this ye may see that it is wisdom for a man to do good deeds himself while he is here, and not to trust to the prayer and promise of his executors.

A.20: *Of the merchaunte that charged his sonne to fynde one to synge for hys soule.*
B.22: *Of the merchaunte that chargyd hys sonne to fynde one to synge for hys sowle.*
D.14: *Marchant that charged, &c.*

charged: commanded, engaged.

unthrifty: profligate, spendthrift (2, 4).

conditions: attitudes, habits (5).

find one daily to sing for him: it was common to leave a bequest for chantry priests to sing Mass regularly for the soul of the deceased, to allow its early release from Purgatory (7-8).

The moral here is similar to that for Tale 28.

From *Summa Praedicantium* by John of Bromyard (d.1352) and *Super Libros Sapientiae* by Robert of Holcot (d.1349).

23. Of the maid washing clothes that answered the friar.

THERE was a maid stood by a river's side in her smock washing clothes. And as she stooped, oft-times her smock cleaved between her buttocks.

By whom there came a friar seeing her, and said in sport, 'Maid, maid, take heed, for Bayard bites on the bridle.'

'Nay wis, Master Friar,' quod the maiden, 'he doth but wipe his mouth, and weeneth ye will come and kiss him.'

By this ye may see that a woman's answer is never to seek.

A.21: *Of the mayde wasshynge clothes that answered the frere.*
B.23: *Of the mayd washyng clothys and answered the frere.*

maid: an unmarried woman (1, 5).

smock: a woman's undershirt (3).

Bayard: a proper name for a bay horse; ultimately derived from Continental legends of a magical horse, in English literature the name is usually used facetiously (5).

wis: certainly, indeed—a variant of 'iwis' (7).

weeneth: supposes, expects, hopes (8).

a woman's answer is never to seek: i.e. a woman has a ready answer for anything so there is no need to go looking for it, with a secondary meaning that it is not to be looked for because it won't be what you want to hear—*cf.* Tale 29 'Of the gentleman that wished his tooth in the gentlewoman's tail' and Tale 58 'Of the wife that bade her husband eat the candle first' (9).

The moral is one of several concerned with the nature and status of women, *cf.* Tales 3, 10, 11, 19, 29, 35, 46, 49, 58, 66 and 97.

24. Of the three wise men of Gotham.

A CERTAIN man there was dwelling in a town called Gotham, which went to a fair three mile off to buy sheep, and as he came over a bridge, he met with one of his neighbours and told him whither he went. And he asked him which way he would bring them. Which said he would bring them over the same bridge.

'Nay,' quod the other man, 'but thou shalt not!'

'By God,' quod he, 'but I will!'

The other again said he should not, and he again said he would bring them over, spite of his teeth, and so fell at words and at the last to buffets, that each one knocked other well about the heads with their fists. To whom there came a third man, which was a miller with a sack of meal upon a horse, a neighbour of theirs, and parted them and asked them what was the cause of their variance, which then showed him the matter and cause, as ye have heard.

This third man, the miller, thought to rebuke their foolishness with a familiar example, and took his sack of meal from his horse back, and opened it and poured all the meal in the sack over the bridge into the running river, whereby all the meal was lost, and said thus:

'By my troth, neighbours, because ye strive for driving over the bridge those sheep which be not yet bought, nor wot not where they be, methinketh therefore there is even as much wit in your heads as there is meal now in my sack.' 25

This tale showeth you that some man taketh upon him to show other men wisdom, when he is but a fool himself.

A.22: *Of the thre wyse men of Gotam.*
B.24: *Of the .iii. wyse men of gotam.*

Gotham: Gotham, Nottinghamshire—the English place name Gotham is pronounced /goʊtəm/ or 'Goat-em' (2).

wot: know (25).

methinketh: it seems to me (25).

This tale is one of many stories of the Wise Men of Gotham, who are supposed to have feigned madness to avoid the wrath of King John. Similar stories must have been associated with Gotham at least as early as the fifteenth century, when the Wakefield Mystery Plays refer to the 'fools of Gotham'—earlier stories in a similar vein are told about the men of Norfolk in the twelfth-century Latin *Descriptio Norfolciensium*. This is the only such story among the *Hundred Merry Tales*, and is the earliest known example of the tradition as it relates to Gotham. The same jest appears as the first tale of *The Merry Tales of the Mad Men of Gotham*, published in 1540 by Andrew Boorde:

There was two men of Gotham, and the one was going to the market at Nottingham to buy sheep and the other did come from the market, and both met together upon Nottingham Bridge.

'Well met,' said the one to the other.

'Whither be you going?' said he that came from Nottingham to him that went to Nottingham.

'Marry,' said he that went to Nottingham, 'I go to the market to buy sheep.'

'Buy sheep?' said the other, 'And which way will you bring them?'

'Marry,' said the other, 'I will bring them over this bridge.'

'By Robin Hood!' said he that came from Nottingham, 'but thou shalt not.'

'By Maid Marion!' said he that went to the market, 'but I will.'

'Thou shalt not,' said the other. 'I will,' said the other.

'Let here,' said the one and, 'Show there,' said the other.

They beat their staves against the ground one against the other, as there had been an hundred sheep betwixt them.

'Hold in there,' said one.

'Beware of the leaping over the bridge of my sheep,' said the other.

'I care not,' said the other, 'they shall not come this way, by the Mass!'

'By the Mass,' said the other, 'but they shall!'

Then said the one, 'And thou make much to-do, I will put my finger in thy mouth.'

'A turd thou wilt!' said the other.

And as they were at this contention, another man of Gotham did come from the market with a sack of meal upon an horse. And seeing and hearing his neighbours at strife for sheep and none betwixt them, said, 'Ah, fools! Will you never learn wit? Help me,' said he that had the meal, 'and lay my sack upon my shoulder.'

They did so, and he went to the one side of the bridge and unloosed the mouth of the sack, and did shake out all his meal into the river.

'Now neighbour,' said this man, 'How much meal is there in my sack now?'

'Marry, there is none at all,' said they.

'Now, by my faith,' said he, 'even as much wit is in your two heads, to strive for that thing which you have not.'

Which was the wisest of all these three persons, judge you?

25. Of the Grey Friar that answered his penitent.

A MAN there was that came to confess himself to a Grey Friar and shrove him that he had lain with a young gentlewoman. The friar then asked him in what place, and he said it was in a goodly chamber, all night long, in a soft, warm bed.

The friar hearing that, shrugged in his clothes and said, 'Now, by sweet St Francis, then wast thou very well at ease.'

A.23: *Of the graye frere that answered his penytente.*
B.25: *Of the gray frere that answeryd his penytent.*

Grey Friar: a member of the Franciscan Order, so called because of their grey habit (2).

shrove: confessed (2).

shrugged: fidgeted (6).

Although the purpose of Confession is to absolve the penitent of sin, here instead the confessor is tempted into sin.

26. Of the gentleman that bore the segboard on his neck.

A CHANDLER being a widower dwelling at Holborn Bridge in London, had a fair daughter whom a young gentleman of Thavie's Inn wooed sore to have his pleasure of her. Which, by long suit to her made, at the last granted him, and appointed him to come upon a night to her father's house in the evening, and she would convey him into her chamber secretly, which was an inner chamber within her father's chamber.

So, according to the appointment, all thing was performed so that he lay with her all night, and made good cheer till about four o'clock in the morning, at which time it fortuned this young gentleman fell a-coughing, which came upon him so sore that he could not refrain.

This young wench then fearing her father that lay in the next chamber, bade him go put his head in the draught lest that her father should hear him. Which, after her counsel, rose in his shirt and so did, but then because of the savour of the draught, it caused him to cough much more and louder, that the wench's father heard it, and asked of his daughter what man it was that coughed in her chamber.

She answered and said, 'Nobody.'

But ever this young man coughed still more and more, whom the father hearing said, 'By God's body, whore, thou liest! I will see who is there,' and rose out of his bed.

This wench perceiving her father rising, came to the gentleman and said, 'Take heed, sir, to yourself, for my father cometh!'

This gentleman, suddenly therewith abashed, would have pulled his head out of the draught hole, which was very strait for his head, that he pulled the segboard up therewith, and hanging about his neck, ran upon the father being an old man, and gave him a great fall and bore him down and hurt his arm, and opened the doors and ran into the street, with the draught board about his neck, toward Thavie's Inn as fast as he could.

This wench for fear ran out of her father's house and came not there a month after.

This gentleman, as he ran upon Holborn Bridge, met with a collier's cart laden with coals, where there was two or three skittish horses which, when they saw this gentleman running, start aside and threw down the cart with coals and drew it aside and broke the cart rope, whereby the coals fell out, some in one place some in another. And after, the horses broke their traces and ran, some toward Smithfield and some toward Newgate, that the collier ran after them, and was an hour and more ere he could get his horse together again. By which time, the

50 people of the street were risen, and came to the street and
saw it strewn with coals. Every one for his part gathered
up the coals, that the most part of the coals were gone ere
the collier had got his horses.

But during this while, the gentleman went through St
55 Andrews Churchyard toward Thavie's Inn, and there met
with the sexton coming to church to ring to Morrow
Mass. Which, when he saw the gentleman in the
churchyard in his shirt with the draught board about his
neck, had weened it had been a spirit and cried, 'Alas, alas,
60 a spirit!' and ran back again to his house almost at The
Bars, and for fear was almost out of his wit, that he was the
worse half a year after.

This gentleman then, because Thavie's Inn Gates were
not open, went on the back side and leapt over the garden
65 wall but, in leaping, the segboard so troubled him that he
fell down into the garden and had almost broken his neck,
and there he lay still till that the principal came into the
garden. Which when he saw him lie there, had weened
some man had been slain and there cast over the wall,
70 and durst not come nigh him till he had called up his
company. Which, when many of the gentlemen were
come together, looked well upon him and knew him,
and after relieved him. But the board that was about his
neck caused his head so to swell, that they could not get it
75 off till they were fain to cut it off with hatchets.

Thus was the wench well japed and for fear she ran
from her father, her father's arm was hurt, the collier lost
his coals, the sexton was almost out of his wit, and the
gentleman had almost broke his neck.

A.24: *Of the gentylman that bare the sege borde on hys necke.*
B.26: *Of the gentylman that bare the sege borde on his nek.*
D.15: *Of the Gentelman that bare.*

segboard, draught board: the seat of a privy or latrine ('seg'), a toilet seat (32, 36, *et al.*).

chandler: a candle maker (1).

Holborn Bridge: the old bridge over the River Fleet, which stood where Holborn Viaduct stands today (1-2, 40).

Thavie's Inn: one of the medieval Inns of Chancery, providing offices and accommodation for young lawyers (3, *et al.*).

draught: a privy (16, 19).

the savour of the draught: the stench from the privy (19).

suddenly: instantly, immediately (30).

abashed: perturbed, disconcerted (30).

start: jumped, leaped, flinched (43).

Smithfield: now principally famous for its meat market, in Rastell's day Smithfield was also a place of execution (47).

Newgate: one of London's historic city gates, Newgate once stood on Newgate Street near the Old Bailey, where it housed an important prison (47).

ere: before (48).

St Andrew's Churchyard: St Andrew Holborn was closely connected with nearby Thavie's Inn; although the church was largely rebuilt in the seventeenth century, the medieval tower remains to this day (55).

sexton: the person who looks after the church and churchyard (56, 78).

Morrow Mass: morning mass, celebrated at prime or terce (56-7).

The Bars: Holborn Bars; the present timber-framed buildings at 1-4 Holborn Bars and 337-8 High Holborn were not built until after Rastell's death, and their medieval forerunners may have been somewhat simpler in style (60-1).

weened: supposed, imagined (59, 68).

durst: dared (70).

well japed: thoroughly mocked (76).

27.   Of the merchant's wife that said she would take a nap at a sermon.

A MERCHANT'S wife there was in Bow Parish in London, somewhat steeped in age, to whom her maid came on a Sunday in Lent after dinner and said, 'Mistress,' quod she, 'they ring at St Thomas of Acres, for
5   there shall be a sermon preached anon.'

To whom the mistress answered and said, 'Marry, God's blessing have thy heart for warning me thereof, and because I slept not well all this night, I pray thee bring my stole with me, for I will go thither to look whether I can
10   take a nap there while the priest is preaching.'

By this ye may see that many one goeth to church as much for other things as for devotion.

A.25: *Of the merchantes wyfe that sayd she wolde take a nap at a sermon.*
B.27: *Of the marchauntys wyfe that seyd she wolde take a nap at sermon.*
D.16: *Of the Marchants wyfe, &c.*

maid: an unmarried female servant (3).

St Thomas of Acre: the medieval church and hospital of St Thomas of Acre on Cheapside marked the birthplace of St Thomas Beckett, and became closely associated with the Mercers' Company; it was destroyed in the Great Fire of 1666 (4).

anon: soon, presently, shortly (5).

marry: indeed, certainly (6).

stole: a robe or shawl (9).

Hugh Latimer included this jest in his sixth sermon before Edward VI on 12th April 1549:
 I had rather ye should come of a naughty mind to hear the word of God, for novelty, or for curiosity to hear some pastime, than to be away. I had rather ye should come as the tale is by the Gentlewoman of London:
 One of her neighbours met her in the street and said, 'Mistress, whither go ye?'
 'Marry,' said she, 'I am going to St Thomas of Acre's to the sermon. I could not sleep all this last night, and I am going now thither—I never failed of a good nap there!'
 And so I had rather ye should go a-napping to the sermons than not to go at all. For with what mind so ever ye come, though ye come for an ill purpose, yet peradventure ye may chance to be caught ere ye go; the preacher may chance to catch you on his hook!

28. Of the woman that said, and she lived another year she would have a cuckold's hat of her own.

THERE was a certain company of women gathered together in communication. One happened thus to say that her pigs, after they were farrowed, died and would not live. And one old wife of her acquaintance, hearing her say so, bade her get a cuckold's hat and put the pigs therein a while after they were farrowed, and they should live.

Which wife, intending to do after her counsel, came to one of her gossips and showed her what medicine was taught her for her pigs, and prayed her to lend her her husband's hat. Which answered her angrily and said, 'I would thou knewest it, drab, I have none. For my husband is no cuckold, for I am a good woman.'

And so likewise, every woman answered her in like manner, that she departed from many of them in anger and scolding. But when she saw she could get none, she came again to her gossip's all angrily and said, 'I have gone round about to borrow a cuckold's hat and I can get none. Wherefore if I live another year, I will have one of mine own, and be out of my neighbours' danger.'

By this tale a man may learn that it is more wisdom for a man to trust more to his own store than to his neighbours' gentleness.

A.26: *Of the woman that said and she lyued another yere she wolde haue a cockoldes hatte of her owne.*

B.28: *Of the woman that seyd & she lyffyd a nother yere she wolde haue a kokoldis hat of her owne.*

D.17: *Of the woman that said, &c.*

and she lived: if she lived.

cuckold: a man with an unfaithful wife (5, *et al.*).

cuckold's hat: the word 'cuckold' may derive from Latin *cuculla*, a medieval hood or cowl, but a 'cuckold's hat' might also have suggested the cockle hat worn by pilgrims which could be adorned with a scallop or cockle shell (5, 18).

farrowed: born (used only of pigs) (3, 6).

gossip: a godparent or godchild, a close friend or companion (9, 17).

I would thou knewest it: I'd like you to know, I'll have you know (12).

drab: harlot, slut (12).

danger: control, power, obligation (20).

The moral here is similar to that for Tale 22.

29. Of the gentleman that wished his tooth in the gentlewoman's tail.

A GENTLEMAN and a gentlewoman sat together talking, which gentleman had great pain in one of his teeth, and happened to say to the gentlewoman thus: 'Iwis, mistress, I have a tooth in my head which grieveth me very sore, wherefore I would it were in your tail.'

She hearing him saying so, answered thus:

'In good faith, sir, if your tooth were in my tail, it could do it but little good, but if there be anything in my tail that can do your tooth good, I would it were in your tooth.'

By this ye may see that a woman's answer is seldom to seek.

A.27: *Of the gentylman that wysshed his tothe in the gentylwomans tayle.*
B.29: *Of the gentylman that wyshyd his toth in the gentylwomans tayle.*
D.18: *Of the Gentelman that &c.*

iwis: certainly, indeed (4).

in your tail: a figure of speech, by which he wishes the pain gone; the gentleman is using the straightforward literal meaning of 'tail' knowing that the gentlewoman has none, but her answer suggests its common colloquial meaning (5).

a woman's answer is seldom to seek: i.e. a woman has a ready answer for anything so there is no need to go looking for it, with a secondary meaning that it is not to be looked for because it won't be what you want to hear—*cf.* Tale 23 'Of the maid washing clothes that answered the friar' and Tale 58 'Of the wife that bade her husband eat the candle first' (10).

The moral is one of several concerned with the nature and status of women, *cf.* Tales 3, 10, 11, 19, 23, 35, 46, 49, 58, 66 and 97.

The punchline of this tale is borrowed by Shakespeare for Petruchio in *The Taming of the Shrew* (c.1590-2), Act II, scene i:

PETRUCHIO: Who knows not where a wasp does wear his sting?
   In his tail.
KATHERINE: In his tongue.
PETRUCHIO: Whose tongue?
KATHERINE: Yours, if you talk of tales. And so farewell.
PETRUCHIO: What, with my tongue in your tail? Nay, come again,
   Good Kate. I am a gentleman.

30. Of the Welshman that confessed him how he had slain a friar.

IN the time of Lent, a Welshman came to be confessed of his curate, which in his confession said that he had killed a friar, to whom the curate said he could not absolve him.

5   'Yes,' quod the Welshman, 'if thou knewest all, thou wouldst absolve me well enough.'

And when the curate commanded him to show him all the case, he said thus:

'Marry, there were two friars and I might have slain
10   them both if I had list, but I let the one scape. Therefore, Master Curate, set the t'one against the t'other, and then the offence is not so great but ye may absolve me well enough.'

By this ye may see that diverse men have so evil and large
15   *confessions that they think, if they do one good deed or refrain from the doing of one evil sin, that it is a satisfaction for other sins and offences.*

A.28: *Of the Welcheman that confessyd hym howe he had slayne a frere.*
B.30: *Of the welchman that confessyd hym how be had slayne a frere.*

curate: a priest charged with the cure or care of souls, a parish priest (2, *et al.*).

marry: indeed, certainly (9).

list: to please or be pleased, to wish, to choose (10).

scape: escape (10).

the t'one against the t'other: the one against the other, possibly reflecting Midland speech—see also Tale 32 'Of the gentlewoman that said to a gentleman, 'Ye have a beard above and none beneath." (11).

31.   Of the Welshman that could not get but a little mail.

THERE was a company of gentlemen in Northampton-shire, which went to hunt for deer in the purlieus in the Gullet beside Stony Stratford. Among which gentlemen there was one which had a Welshman to his servant, a good archer. Which, when they came to a place where they thought they should have game, they made a standing and appointed this Welshman to stand by a tree nigh the highway, and bade him in any wise to take heed that he shot at no rascal nor meddle not without it were a male. And if it were a male, to spare not.

'Well,' quod this Welshman, 'Let me alone.'

And when this Welshman had stand there awhile, he saw much deer coming, as well of antler as of rascal, but ever he let them go and took no heed to them. And within an hour after, he saw come riding in the highway a man of the country, which had a budget hanging at his saddle bow. And when this Welshman had espied him, he bade him stand and began to draw his bow, and bade him deliver that little mail that hung at his saddle bow.

This man for fear of his life was glad to deliver him his 20
budget and so did, and then rode his way and was glad he
was so escaped. And when this man of the country was
gone, this Welshman was very glad and went incontinent
to seek his master and, at the last, found him with his
company, and when he saw him, he came to him and 25
said thus:

'Master, by Cot's Plut and Her Nail, I have stand yonder
this two hours, and I could see never a mail but a little
mail that a man had hanging at his saddle bow, and that I
have gotten and lo, here it is!' and took his master the 30
budget which he had taken away from the foresaid man,
for the which deed both the master and the servant were
afterward in great trouble.

By this ye may learn it is great folly for a master to put a
servant to that business whereof he can nothing skill and 35
wherein he hath not been used.

mail: bag; the Welshman mistakes the technical term 'male' (now in more common usage) for the common sixteenth-century word 'mail' meaning 'bag' (19, *et al.*).

purlieu: an area on the edge of a royal forest where hunting was not controlled by forest law (2).

the Gullet: near Whittlebury, Northamptonshire, in the purlieus of Whittlewood Forest; Whittlewood was the forest closest to Rastell's home town of Coventry (3).

Stony Stratford: Stony Stratford, Buckinghamshire; this town was an important staging post on the road to London from Coventry (3).

standing: a place to stand and shoot game (7).

rascal: a young deer without antlers, also used for a lean and scrawny deer (9, 13).

meddle: to do something, to busy or exert oneself (9).

without it were: unless it were (9).

male: i.e. a male deer, a stag; this word was less common in sixteenth-century usage, which leads to the Welshman's confusion (10).

let me alone: leave me to it (11).

antler: an older male deer with antlers, a buck or stag (13).

budget: a kind of bag commonly used by travellers, similar to a 'mail' (16, *et al.*).

saddle bow: the bow-shaped front of the saddle (16-7).

incontinent: straight away, immediately (23).

By Cot's Plut and Her Nail: By God's Blood and His [Crucifixion] Nail—in imitation of the Welshman's accent (27).

can nothing skill: has no ability (35).

wherein he hath not been used: in which he has no experience (36).

32. Of the gentlewoman that said to a gentleman, 'Ye have a beard above and none beneath.'

A YOUNG gentleman of the age of twenty year, somewhat disposed to mirth and game, on a time talked with a gentlewoman which was right wise and also merry. This gentlewoman, as she talked with
5 him happened to look upon his beard, which was but young and somewhat grown upon the over lip and but little grown beneath, as all other young men's beards commonly use to grow, and said to him thus:

'Sir, ye have a beard above and none beneath.'

10 And he, hearing her say so, said in sport, 'Mistress, ye have a beard beneath and none above.'

'Marry,' quod she, 'then set the t'one against the t'other!'

Which answer made the gentleman so abashed that he had not one word to answer.

A.30: *Of the gentyll woman that sayde to a gentyll man ye haue a berde aboue and none benethe.*
B.32: *Of the gentyll woman that sayd to a gentylman ye haue a berde a boue and none benethe.*
D.19: The Gentilman that said, &c.

use to grow: are accustomed to grow (8).

marry: indeed, certainly (12).

the t'one against the t'other: the one against the other, possibly reflecting Midland speech—see Tale 30 'Of the Welshman that confessed him how be had slain a friar' (12).

abashed: disconcerted, embarrassed (13).

33. Of the friar that said Our Lord fed five thousand people with two fishes.

THERE was a certain White Friar which was a very glutton and a great niggard, which had an ungracious boy that ever followed him and bore his cloak. And what for the friar's gluttony and for his churlishness, the boy where he went could scant get meat enough, for the friar would eat almost all himself.

But on a time, the friar made a sermon in the country, wherein he touched very many miracles which Christ did afore his Passion, among which he specially rehearsed the miracle which Christ did in feeding five thousand people with five loaves of bread and with two little fishes. And this friar's boy, which cared not greatly for his master, hearing him say so and considering that his master was so great a churl and glutton, answered with a loud voice that all the church heard and said, 'By my troth, Master, then there were no friars there!'

Which answer made all the people to fall on such a laughing that for shame the friar went out of the pulpit. And as for the friar's boy, he then departed out of the church that the friar never saw him after.

By this ye may see that it is honesty for a man that is at meat to depart with such as he has to them that be present.

A.31: *Of the frere that sayde our Lorde fed fyue M. people with iii fysshys.*
B.33: *Of the frere that sayd our lord fed .v. M peple with .ij. fyshys.*
D.20: *The freir that said our, &c.*

White Friar: a member of the Carmelite Order, so called because of their white cloaks (1).

very: veritable, true (1).

niggard: miser (*cg.* ON *nigla*, to niggle, to fuss over little things) (2).

ungracious: graceless, rude (2).

to depart with: to divide or share out (22).

The moral is one of several concerned with covetousness, miserliness, and attitudes to money and personal possessions, *cf.* Tales 15, 17, 20, 62, 68, 78, 90, 91 and 100.

34. Of the franklin that would have had the friar gone.

A RICH franklin dwelling in the country had a friar using to his house of whom he could never be rid, and had tarried with him the space of a seven-night and would never depart. Wherefore the franklin, being weary of him, on a time as he and his wife and this friar sat together at supper, feigned himself very angry with his wife, insomuch he said he would beat her.

This friar, perceiving well what they meant, said thus: 'Master Franklin, I have been here this seven-night when ye were friends, and I will tarry here this fortnight longer, but I will see you friends again ere I go.'

This man, perceiving that he could no good nor would not depart by none honest means, answered him shortly and said, 'By God, friar, but thou shalt abide here no longer!' and took him by the shoulders and thrust him out of the doors by violence.

By this ye may see that he that will learn no good by example nor good manner to him showed is worthy to be taught with open rebukes.

A.32: *Of the frankelyn that wold haue had the frere gone.*
B.34: *Of the frankelyne that wold haue had the frere gon.*
D.21: *The Franklin that wold, &c.*

franklin: a free landowner—one step down from a gentleman (1, *et al.*).

using to his house: frequenting or staying at his house (2).

seven-night: a week (3, 9).

ere: before (11).

could no good: was unable to do good, or unable to recognise good (12).

shortly: promptly, briskly (13).

The moral is among several which contrast wisdom, learning and orderly behaviour with foolishness, wilfulness and stupidity, *cf.* Tales 1, 5, 8, 37, 67, 69, 71, 73, 75 and 81.

35. Of the goodman that said to his wife he had ill fare.

A FRIAR Limiter came into a poor man's house in the country, and because this poor man thought this friar might do him some good, he therefore thought to make him good cheer. But because his wife would dress him no good meat for cost, he therefore at dinnertime said thus:

'By God, wife, because thou didst dress me no good meat to my dinner, were it not for Master Friar, thou shouldst have half a dozen stripes!'

'Nay, sir!' quod the friar. 'I pray you spare not for me.'

Wherewith the wife was angry, and therefore at supper she caused them to fare worse.

By this ye may see it is good policy for guests, if they will have any good cheer, to please alway the wife of the house.

goodman: husband.

limiter: a friar who paid his convent a fee for the exclusive right to beg within the limits of a fixed district (1).

would dress him no good meat for cost: would not cook him any good meat, because of the expense (4-5).

stripes: lashes or blows from a whip or rod, or the marks or weals left by such lashes (9).

The moral is one of several concerned with the nature and status of women, *cf.* Tales 3, 10, 11, 19, 23, 29, 46, 49, 58, 66 and 97.

36. Of the friar that bade his child make a Latin.

THERE was a friar which, though he were well learned, yet he was called wicked of conditions, which had a gentleman's son to wait upon him and to teach him to speak Latin.

5   This friar came to this child's father dwelling in the country, and because this friar would have this gentleman to know that this child had meetly well spent his time for the while he had been with him, he bade this child to make in Latin shortly, 'Friars walk in the cloister.'

10   This child, half astonished because his master bade him make this Latin so shortly, answered at all adventures and said, '*In circuitu impii ambulant.*'

A.35: *Of the frere that bad his childe make a laten.*
B.36: *Of the frere that bad hys chylde make a laten.*

wicked of conditions: wicked by nature or disposition (2).

gentleman: a lord of the manor—one step down from a knight or esquire (3, 6).

meetly: appropriately, properly (7).

friars walk in the cloister: the sort of stock phrase traditionally set for translation when teaching languages (9).

shortly: quickly, hastily (9, 11).

at all adventures: regardless, no matter what (11).

in circuitu impii ambulant: 'the wicked ramble around'—suggesting the ramblings of mendicant friars (12).

37. Of the gentleman that asked the friar for his bearer.

IN the term time, a good old gentleman being a lawyer came to London to the term, and as he came he happened to overtake a friar which was some unthrift and went alone without his bearer. Wherefore this gentleman asked this friar where was his bearer that should keep him company, and said it was contrary to his religion to go alone, and it would cause people to suppose him to be some apostate or some unthrift.

'By God, sir,' quod the friar, 'my fellow commendeth him unto your mastership.'

'Why!' quod the gentleman, 'I know him not.'

'Then,' quod the friar to the gentleman, 'ye are the more to blame to ask for him.'

By this tale ye may see that he that giveth counsel to an unthrift and teacheth him his duty shall have oftentimes but a mock for his labour.

A.36: *Of the gentylman that asked the frere for his beuer.*
B.37: *Of the gentylman that askyd the frere for his beuer.*

bearer: the boy or servant accompanying the friar (*cf.* Tales 33, 36, 51 and 57) —both Rastell's editions read 'beuer' throughout this tale, which may be a misreading of 'berer' in a source manuscript (4, 5).

in the term time: the English legal year is traditionally divided into four terms—Michaelmas, Hilary, Easter, and Trinity; there are breaks between the terms, with the longest being between the end of Trinity Term in July and the start of the new legal year with Michaelmas Term in October (1).

unthrift: good-for-nothing (3).

The moral is among several which contrast wisdom, learning and orderly behaviour with foolishness, wilfulness and stupidity, *cf.* Tales 1, 5, 8, 34, 67, 69, 71, 73, 75 and 81.

38.   Of the three men
that chose the woman.

THREE gentlemen came into an inn where a fair woman was tapster, wherefore as these three sat there making merry, each one of them kissed her and made good pastime and pleasure.

5 Howbeit, one spoke merrily and said, 'I cannot see how this gentlewoman is able to make pastime and pleasure to us all three, except that she were departed in three parts.'

'By my troth,' quod one of them, 'if that she might be so departed, then I would choose for my part her head and

10 her fair face, that I might alway kiss her.'

Then quod the second, 'I would have the breast and heart, for there lieth her love.'

Then quod the third, 'Then there is nothing left for me but the loins, buttocks and legs, and I am content to have

15 it for my part.'

And when these gentlemen had passed the time there by the space of one hour or two, they took their leave and were going away but, ere they went, the third man that had chosen the belly and the buttocks did kiss the tapster and

20 bade her farewell.

'What!' quod the first man that had chosen the face and the mouth, 'Why dost thou so? Thou dost me wrong to kiss my part that I have chosen of her.'

'Oh,' quod the other, 'I pray thee be not angry, for I am

25 content that thou shalt kiss my part for it.'

A.37: *Of the thre men that chose the woman.*
B.38: *Of the .iii. men that chase the woman.*

tapster: a woman who taps ale from the barrel, a barmaid (2, 19).

departed: divided, split (7, 9).

ere: before (18).

39. Of the gentleman that taught his cook the medicine for the toothache.

IN Essex there dwelled a merry gentleman which had a cook called Thomas, that was greatly diseased with the toothache and complained to his master thereof. Which said he had a book of medicines, and said he
5 would look up his book to see whether he could find any medicine therein for it, and so sent one of his daughters to his study for his book, and incontinent looked upon it a long season and then said thus to his cook:

'Thomas,' quod he, 'here is a medicine for your tooth-
10 ache, and it is a charm. But it will do you no good except ye kneel on your knees and ask it for St Charity.'

This man, glad to be released of his pain, kneeled and said, 'Master, for St Charity, let me have that medicine.'

Then quod this gentleman, 'Kneel on your knees, and
15 say after me.' Which kneeled down and said after him as he bade him.

This gentleman began, and said thus:

'The sun on the Sunday.'

'The sun on the Sunday,' quod Thomas.
20 'The moon on the Monday.'

'The moon on the Monday.'

'The Trinity on the Tuesday.'

'The Trinity on the Tuesday.'

'The wit on the Wednesday.'
25 'The wit on the Wednesday.'

154

'The holy, holy Thursday.'
'The holy, holy Thursday.'
'And all that fast on Friday.'
'And all that fast on Friday.'
'Shit in thy mouth on Saturday.'   30

This Thomas, cook, hearing his master thus mocking him, in an anger start up and said, 'By God's Body, mocking churl, I will never do thee service more,' and went forth to his chamber to get his gear together, to the intent to have gone thence by and by.   35

But what for the anger that he took with his master for the mock that he gave him, and what for labour that he took to gather his gear so shortly together, the pain of the toothache went from him incontinent, that his master came to him and made him to tarry still, and told him that   40 his charm was the cause of the ease of the pain of his toothache.

By this tale ye may see that anger oft times putteth away the bodily pain.

A.38: *Of the gentylman that taught his cooke the medycyne for the tothake.*
B.39: *Of the gentylman that taught his cooke the medesyne for the tothake.*
D.22: *The Gentelman that, &c.*

incontinent: straight away, immediately (7, 39).

St Charity: the sisters Faith, Hope and Charity are reputed to have been martyrs in Ancient Rome; their names represent the three key virtues required in the First Epistle to the Corinthians, 1 Corinthians 13 (11, 13).

shortly: hastily, quickly (38).

40. Of the gentleman that promised the scholar of Oxford a sarcenet tippet.

A SCHOLAR of Oxford lately made Master of Arts came to the City of London and in Paul's met with the said merry gentleman of Essex which was ever disposed to play many merry pageants, with whom
5 before he had been of familiar acquaintance, and prayed him to give him a sarcenet tippet. This gentleman, more liberal of promise than of gift, granted him he should have one if he would come to his lodging to the sign of the Bull without Bishop's Gate in the next morning at
10 six of the clock.

This scholar thanked him, and for that night departed to his lodging in Fleet Street. And in the morning early as he appointed, came to him to the sign of the Bull. Anon as this gentleman saw him, he bade him go with
15 him into the City and he should be sped anon, which incontinent went together till he came into St Lawrence Church in the Jewry, where the gentleman espied a priest ravished to Mass, and told the scholar that 'yonder is the priest that hath the tippet for you,' and bade him kneel
20 down in the pew and he would speak to him for it. And incontinent, this gentleman went to the priest and said, 'Sir, here is a scholar and kinsman of mine, greatly diseased with the chin cough. I pray you, when Mass is done, give him three draughts of your chalice.'

The priest granted him, and turned him to the scholar and said, 'Sir, I shall serve you as soon as I have said Mass.'

The scholar then tarried still and heard the Mass, trusting then, when the Mass was done, that the priest would give him his tippet of sarcenet. This gentleman in the meanwhile departed out of the church.

This priest when Mass was done, put wine in the chalice and came to the scholar kneeling in the pew, proffering him to drink of the chalice. This scholar looked upon him and mused and said, 'Why, Master Parson, wherefore proffer ye me the chalice?'

'Marry,' quod the priest, 'for the gentleman told me ye were diseased with the chin cough, and prayed me therefore that for a medicine ye might drink of the chalice.'

'Nay, by St Mary,' quod the scholar, 'he promised me ye should deliver me a tippet of sarcenet.'

'Nay,' said the priest, 'he spoke to me of no tippet, but he desired me to give you drink of the chalice for the chin cough.'

'By God's Body,' quod the scholar, 'he is, as he was ever wont to be, but a mocking wretch. And ever I live, I shall quite it him,' and so departed out of the church in great anger.

By this tale ye may perceive it is no wisdom for a man to trust to a man to do a thing that is contrary to his old accustomed conditions.

A.39: *Of the gentylman that promysed the scoler of Oxford a sarcenet typet.*
B.40: *Of the gentylman that promysyd the scoler of Oxford a sarcenet typet.*

sarcenet: a fine silken cloth, shot silk taffeta (6, *et al.*).

tippet: a shoulder cape (an item of academic dress); an Act of 1533 for the Reformation of Excess in Apparel allowed bachelors of divinity and doctors to use sarcenet, black velvet or satin in their tippets (6, *et al.*).

Paul's: St Paul's Cathedral (2).

the said merry gentleman: see the previous tale, Tale 39 'Of the gentleman that taught his cook the medicine for the toothache' (3).

merry pageants: pranks, practical jokes (4).

the sign of the Bull: the Black Bull on Bishopsgate would later be a venue for the Queen's Men, and may already have been associated with players in Rastell's day (8-9).

without Bishop's Gate: outside the City Walls near Bishop's Gate, one of the medieval entries to London, in the north east of the city (9).

Fleet Street: Fleet Street was known for its plentiful taverns and hostelries (12).

anon: soon, presently, shortly (14).

sped: fixed up, sorted, having achieved one's goal (15).

incontinent: straight away, immediately (16, 21).

St Lawrence Church in the Jewry: the medieval church of St Lawrence Jewry on King Street, Cheapside, was destroyed in the Great Fire of 1666; Old Jewry had been occupied by English Jews before their expulsion in 1290 (16-7).

ravished to Mass: caught up with or intent upon the celebration of Mass (18).

chin cough: whooping cough (23, *et al.*).

marry: indeed, certainly (36).

medicine: the wine in the chalice has been consecrated for use in the Mass (38).

and ever: if ever (46).

quite: requite, make quits (47).

A somewhat different version of the same tale is told in the *Jests of Scoggin* (1565-6):

When Scoggin should be made Master of Art, he wanted money to buy his apparel, and he mused in his mind what shift he might make. At last, he went to London to a draper and said, 'Sir, it is so, that I have a master which is Dean of Wells, and he would have four gown clothes of sundry colours but they must be sad colours and fine cloth, and he must have three pair of hose clothes and lining, and I pray you make me a bill of the price of everything, and tomorrow you shall have money.'

On the morrow in the morning, Scoggin went to Paul's Church and he did see a lusty priest come in with two or three servants, and did ask where he might say mass. And when the place was appointed, Scoggin did run to the draper and said, 'Sir, you must come or send one to receive your money, for my master will say mass and then in all haste he must go to Westminster. Therefore, let one of your servants cut of the cloth.'

The draper and Scoggin went to Paul's, and by that time, the priest had on his alb ready to go to mass. Scoggin went to the priest and said, 'Master, it is so, that I have a friend here which is troubled with a chin cough, and he and I desire you that after mass he may have three sups of the chalice, and for your pains he doth pray you to come to him to breakfast.'

The Priest said, 'I am pleased. I will do your desire.'

Then Scoggin went to the draper and said, 'Sir, come and hear what my master doth say.'

Then Scoggin said to the priest, 'Master, here is the gentleman. Will you dispatch him when mass is done?'

'Yea,' said the priest.

Then said Scoggin, 'Here is your bill of accounts, now send me to your servants, by what token I shall receive that which my master hath bought.'

The draper said, 'By the same token that I did tell them yesternight, that if they would not take heed in time, they should never thrive.'

Upon this token, all the stuff was delivered to Scoggin, and he carried it to the carriers and sent it to Oxford. When the mass was done, the priest called the draper and said, 'Gentleman, come hither to me. If you will have three sups of the chalice, sit down on your knees.'

'Why,' said the draper, 'should I sup of the chalice, and wherefore shall I sit down on my knees?'

'Marry, sir,' said the priest, 'your servant, as I suppose, did come to me before mass, saying that you had the chin cough and that you would have three sups of the chalice to be mended of your disease.'

The draper said, 'Master Dean of Wells, you shall not mock me so. I must have thirteen pounds of you for clothes that your servant hath of me for four gown clothes and three hose clothes and lining for them, and hear is a bill of every parcel, and you said before mass that I should have it.'

'What?' said the priest.

'Money,' said the merchant.

'Nay, not so,' said the priest. 'I am not Dean of Wells, nor I never bought nor sold with you, and you shall have no money of me for I promised nothing before mass but three sups of the chalice, and if thou wilt have that take it, or else fare ye well.'

'A fart for thy three sups of the chalice!' said the draper. 'Give me my money!'

'I owe thee none,' said the priest, 'nor none shalt thou have of me.'

The merchant could not tell what to say, but hied himself home to seek for Scoggin, which was gone. Then said the draper, 'I trow we have spun a fair thread. Where is the man that should have the cloth?'

The servants said, 'Sir, he hath it, and is gone.'

'Which way?' said the merchant.

'We cannot tell,' said his servants.

'Why,' said the draper, 'did you deliver him all the stuff?'

'Yes, sir,' said they, 'because you sent us a true token.'

Then said the draper, 'I would I had been ware myself first, for if I make many such bargains, I shall never thrive.'

41. Of Master Skelton that brought the Bishop of Norwich two pheasants.

IT fortuned there was a great variance between the Bishop of Norwich and one Master Skelton, a Poet Laureate, insomuch that the bishop commanded him that he should not come in at his gates.

5   This Master Skelton did absent himself for a long season, but at the last he thought to do his duty to him, and studied ways how he might obtain the bishop's favour, and determined himself that he would come to him with some present, and humble himself to the
10 bishop, and got a couple of pheasants and came to the bishop's place and required the porter he might come in to speak with my lord.

    This porter, knowing his lord's pleasure, would not suffer him to come in at the gates. Wherefore, this
15 Master Skelton went on the back side, to seek some other way to come in to the place. But the place was moated, that he could see no way to come over except in one place, where there lay a long tree over the moat in manner of a bridge that was fallen down with wind.
20 Wherefore, this Master Skelton went along upon the tree to come over. And when he was almost over, his foot slipped for lack of sure footing, and fell into the moat up to the middle. But at the last, he recovered himself and,

as well as he could, dried himself again, and suddenly came to the bishop, being in his hall then lately risen 25 from dinner. Which, when he saw Skelton coming suddenly said to him, 'Why, thou caitiff, I warned thee thou shouldst never come in at my gates, and charged my porter to keep thee out.'

'Forsooth, my lord,' quod Skelton, 'though ye gave such 30 charge, and though your gates be never so surely kept, yet it is no more possible to keep me out of your doors than to keep out crows or pies, for I came not in at your gates, but I came over the moat, that I have been almost drowned for my labour,' and showed his clothes, how evil 35 he was arrayed, which caused many that stood thereby to laugh apace.

Then quod Skelton, 'If it like your lordship, I have brought you a dish to your supper, a couple of pheasants.'

'Nay,' quod the bishop, 'I defy thee and thy pheasants 40 also. And wretch as thou art, pick thee out of my house, for I will none of thy gift.'

Howbeit, with as humble words as he could, this Skelton desired the bishop to be his good lord, and to take his little gift of him. But the bishop called him 'daw' and 'fool' 45 oftentimes, and in no wise would receive that gift. This Skelton then considering that the bishop called him 'fool' so oft, said to one of his familiars thereby that, though it were evil to be christened a fool, yet it was much worse to

50 be confirmed a fool of such a bishop, for the name of
    confirmation must needs abide. Therefore, he imagined
    how he might avoid that confirmation, and mused a while
    and at the last, said to the bishop thus:

    'If your lordship knew the names of these pheasants,
55 ye would be content to take them.'

    'Why, caitiff,' quod the bishop hastily and angrily,
    'what be their names?'

    'Iwis, my lord,' quod Skelton, 'this pheasant is called
    Alpha, which is *in primus*, 'the first', and this is called
60 Omega, that is *novissimus*, 'the last'. And for the more
    plain understanding of my mind, if it please your
    lordship to take them, I promise you this Alpha is the
    first that ever I gave you, and this Omega is the last that
    ever I will give you while I live.'

65 At the which answer, all that were by made great
    laughter, and all they desired the bishop to be good lord
    unto him for his merry conceits, at whose request ere
    they went, the bishop was content to take him unto his
    favour again.

70 *By this ye may see that merry conceits doth a man much*
    more good than to fret himself with anger and melancholy.

A.40: *Of mayster Skelton that broughte the bysshop of Norwiche ii fesauntys.*
B.41: *Of master skelton that brought the byshop of Norwich .ii. fesantys.*

Master Skelton: John Skelton (c.1463–1529), the celebrated scholar, satirist, poet, and former tutor of Henry VIII, was Rector of Diss, Norfolk, from 1502, but returned to London in 1512, where he may have been an acquaintance of Rastell (2, *et al.*).

a great variance: according to the *Merry Tales of Master Skelton* (1567), Skelton's parishioners had complained to Bishop Nix that he had a son by 'a fair wench' (1).

Bishop of Norwich: Bishop Richard Nix (c.1447–1535, Bishop of Norwich 1501–1535) (2).

place: mansion, palace (11, *et al.*).

suddenly: immediately, unexpectedly (24, 27).

caitiff: wretch, scoundrel (27, 56).

forsooth: indeed, certainly (30).

pies: magpies (33).

how evil he was arrayed: sewage from the palace goes into the moat, and Skelton is now covered in it (35-6).

pick thee: remove yourself (41).

daw: fool, simpleton (45).

iwis: certainly, indeed (58).

Alpha and Omega: the first and last letters of the Greek alphabet which in Christianity are symbolic of God, after Revelation 1:8, 'I am Alpha and Omega, the beginning and the ending, saith the Lord, which is, and which was, and which is to come, the Almighty' (59-60).

conceits: witticisms (67).

ere: before (67).

This story is retold in the *Merry Tales of Master Skelton* (1567):

Skelton did keep a musket [*i.e.* a mistress] at Diss, upon the which he was complained on to the Bishop of Norwich. The bishop sent for Skelton. Skelton did take two capons, to give them for a present to the bishop. And as soon as he had saluted the bishop he said, 'My lord, here I have brought you a couple of capons.'

The bishop was blind and said, 'Who be you?'

'I am Skelton,' said Skelton.

The bishop said, 'A whore head, I will none of thy capons! Thou keepest unhappy rule in thy house, for the which thou shalt be punished.'

'What?' said Skelton. 'Is the wind at that door?' and said, 'God be with you, my lord.' And Skelton with his capons went his way.

The bishop sent after Skelton to come again. Skelton said, 'What? Shall I come again to speak with a madman?'

At last, he returned to the bishop, which said to him, 'I would,' said the bishop, 'that you should not live such a slanderous life that all your parish should not wonder and complain on you as they do. I pray you amend and hereafter live honestly, that I hear no more such words of you. And if you will tarry dinner, you shall be welcome. And I thank you,' said the bishop, 'for your capons.'

Skelton said, 'My lord, my capons have proper names: the one is named Alpha; the other is named Omega. My lord,' said Skelton, 'This capon is named Alpha; this is the first capon that I did ever give to you. And this capon is named Omega, and this is the last capon that ever I will give you. And so, fare you well,' said Skelton.

Another version appears in the *Jests of Scoggin* (1565-6):

There was a bishop in France, which was of the French king's Privy Council. This bishop had a man whose name was Peter Arcadus. This Peter Arcadus favoured Scoggin much because he was so merry, in so much that he got Scoggin to be his chamber-fellow, through whose procuration Scoggin came in favour with the bishop. And on a time, Scoggin in his jesting said that the bishop's nose was so long that he could kiss nobody, for which the bishop was angry and commanded him to come no more within his gates. Then Scoggin went and bought a couple of woodcocks, and because he could not be suffered to come in at the bishop's gate, he got a long pole or rafter, the which he laid over the moat or ditch of the bishop's house, intending to come unto the bishop and give him the woodcocks for a present.

As Scoggin was halfway over, the rafter slipped and he fell into the moat. At last, Scoggin got out, and came in where he found the bishop at dinner and said, 'If it please your honour, here I have brought you a couple of woodcocks.'

The bishop seeing him said, 'Why, thou knave! I commanded thee to come no more within my gates.'

Scoggin said, 'I came not in at your gates, for I came over your moat where I was new christened, and now you have confirmed me a knave, so by this means, I must needs be a knave. Therefore, I desire you my lord, not to be displeased although I play the knave.'

Whereat, the bishop and all that were in the house laughed, and then the bishop said, 'I will pardon you for this time, so that hereafter you will be an honest man.'

42. Of the Yeoman of Guard that said he would beat the carter.

A YEOMAN of the King's Guard dwelling in a village beside London had a very fair young wife, to whom a carter of the town, a tall fellow, resorted and lay with her diverse times when her husband was from home, and so openly known that all the town spoke thereof. Wherefore there was a young man of the town, well acquainted with this Yeoman of Guard, that told him that such a carter had lain by his wife. To whom this Yeoman of Guard said and swore by God's Body, that if he met with him it should cost him his life.

'Marry,' quod the young man, 'if ye go straight even now the high way, ye shall overtake him driving of a cart laden with hay toward London.'

Wherefore this Yeoman of Guard incontinent rode after this carter, and within short space overtook him and knew him well enough, and incontinent called the carter to him and said thus:

'Sirrah, I understand that thou dost lie every night with my wife, when I am from home.'

This carter, being nothing afraid of the other, answered, 'Yea, marry. What then?'

'What then?' quod the Yeoman of Guard. 'By God's Heart, hadst thou not told me the truth, I would have broken thy head.'

And so the Yeoman of Guard returned, and no hurt done nor stroke stricken nor proffered.   25

By this ye may see that the greatest crackers sometime, when it cometh to the proof, be most cowards.

A.41: *Of the yeman of garde that sayd he wolde bete the carter.*
B.42: *Of the yeman of gard that sayd he wold bete the carter.*

Yeoman of the Guard: commonly known as 'Beefeaters,' The King's Body Guard of the Yeomen of the Guard was formed by King Henry VII in 1485, and originally consisted of fifty picked men all over 6ft in height (183cm) (1, *et al.*).

marry: indeed, certainly (11).

incontinent: straight away, immediately (14, 16).

sirrah: a form of address suggesting the speaker's assumed social superiority, just as 'sir' suggests the opposite (18).

cracker: a boaster, a braggart (27).

proof: test (28).

The moral here is similar to that for Tale 76.

43. Of the priest that said Our Lady was not so curious a woman.

IN the town of Botley dwelled a miller which had a good homely wench to his daughter, whom the curate of the next town loved and, as the fame went, had her at his pleasure.

5 But on a time, this curate preached 'of these curious wives nowadays' and, whether it were for the nonce, or whether it came out at all adventures, he happened to say thus in his sermon:

'Ye wives, ye be so curious in all your works that ye
10 wot not what ye mean, but ye should follow Our Lady. For Our Lady was nothing so curious as ye be, but she was a good homely wench, like the miller's daughter of Botley.'

At which saying, all the parishioners made great
15 laughing, and specially they that knew that he loved that same wench.

By this ye may see it is great folly for a man that is suspected with any person, to praise or to name the same person openly, lest it bring him further in slander.

A.33: *Of the prest that sayd Our Lady was not so curyous a woman.*
B.43: *Of the pryst that sayd our lady was not so curyous a woman.*

curious: subtle, sophisticated, delicate (5, *et al.*).

Botley: Botley, Buckinghamshire (1, 13).

homely: simple, innocent, plain (2, 12).

curate: a priest charged with the cure or care of souls, a parish priest; as a priest, he will have taken a vow of chastity, but priests were well known to take mistresses (2, 5).

fame: rumour (3).

for the nonce: for the specific purpose, because it was apt, temporary—from 'Nones', one of the Canonical Hours (6).

at all adventures: heedlessly, inadvertently, no matter what (7).

wot: know (10).

mean: to intend, desire or seek (10).

This tale follows Tale 34 in 'A', but the order is revised in 'B', presumably so that Tales 34 & 35 can be read as a linked pair.

44. Of the fool that said he would go to the Devil.

A FOOL there was, that dwelled with a gentleman in the country which was called a great tyrant and an extortioner. But this fool loved his master marvellously, because he cherished him so well.

5 It happened upon a season, one of the gentleman's servants said to the fool as they talked of sermon matters, 'By my troth, Jack,' quod he, 'would to God that thou and I were both of us in Heaven.'

'Nay, by Lady,' quod the fool, 'I will not go to Heaven, 10 for I had liever go to Hell.'

Then the other asked him why he had liever go to Hell.

'By my troth,' quod the fool, 'for I will go with my master, and I am sure my master shall go to Hell. For every man saith he shall go to the Devil of Hell, and therefore 15 I will go thither with him.'

172

A.42: *Of the fole that saide he had leuer go to hell than to heuen.*
B.44: *Of the fole that wold go to the deuyll.*
D.23: *Of the fule that said he wold.*

gentleman: a lord of the manor—one step down from a knight or esquire (1, 5).

by Lady: by the Virgin Mary, by Our Lady (9).

I will not: I don't want to (9).

liever: rather (10, 11).

I will: I want to (12, 15).

from *Summa Praedicantium* by John of Bromyard (d.1352).

45. Of the ploughman's son that said he saw one make a goose to crake sweetly.

THERE was a certain ploughman's son of the country of the age of sixteen years, that never come much among company but alway went to plough and husbandry.

On a time, this young lad went to a wedding with his father, where he see one lute upon a lute. And when he came home again at night, his mother asked him what sport he had at wedding.

This lad answered and said, 'By my troth, mother,' quod he, 'there was one that brought in a goose between his arms, and tickled her so upon the neck that she craked the sweetliest that ever I heard goose crake in my life.'

A.43: *Of the plowmannys sonne that sayde he sawe one to make a gose to creke swetely.*
B.45: *Of the plowmannys sonne that sayd he saw one make a Gose to kreke sweetly.*
D.24: *The plowmans sone that, &c.*

crake: to croak, cackle or caw (11, 12).

lute upon a lute: to play music on a lute (an expensive stringed instrument) (6).

46. Of the maid's answer that was with child.

IN a merchant's house in London there was a maid which was gotten with child, to whom the mistress of the house came and charged her to tell her who was the father of the child.

5 To whom the maiden answered, 'Forsooth, nobody.'

'Why!' quod the mistress, 'It is not possible but some man must be the father thereof.'

To whom the maid said, 'Why, mistress! Why may I not have a child without a man as well as a hen to lay

10 eggs without a cock?'

Here ye may see it is hard to find a woman without an excuse.

maid, maiden: an unmarried female servant (1, *et al.*).

forsooth: indeed, certainly (5).

it is hard to find a woman without an excuse: this moral is akin to the moral 'a woman's answer is never to seek'—*cf.* Tale 23 'Of the maid washing clothes that answered the friar', Tale 29 'Of the gentleman that wished his tooth in the gentlewoman's tail' and Tale 58 'Of the wife that bade her husband eat the candle first' (11-2).

The moral is one of several concerned with the nature and status of women, *cf.* Tales 3, 10, 11, 19, 23, 29, 35, 49, 58, 66 and 97.

47. Of the servant that rhymed with his master.

A GENTLEMAN there was dwelling nigh Kingston upon Thames, and, riding in the country with his servant, which was not the most quickest fellow but rode alway sadly by his master and had very few words, his
5 master said to him, 'John,' quod he, 'why ridest thou so sadly? I would have thee tell me some merry tales for to pass the time withal.'

'By my troth, master,' quod he, 'I can tell no tales.'

'Why!' quod the master. 'Canst thou not sing?'

10 'No, by my troth,' quod his servant, 'I could never sing in all my life.'

'Why!' quod the master. 'Canst thou rhyme, then?'

'By my troth, master,' quod he, 'I cannot tell, but if ye will begin to rhyme, I will follow as well as I can.'

15 'By my troth,' quod the master, 'that is well said. Then I will begin to make a rhyme. Let me see how well thou canst follow.'

So the master mused a while and then began to rhyme thus: 'Many men's swans swim in Thames, and so do
20 mine.'

Then quod the servant, 'And many a man lieth by other men's wives, and so do I by thine.'

'What dost thou, whoreson?' quod the master.

'By my troth, master, nothing,' quod he, 'but make up the rhyme.'   25

'But,' quod the master, 'I charge thee tell me why thou sayest so.'

'Forsooth, master,' quod he, 'for nothing in the world but to make up your rhyme.'

'Then,' quod the master, 'if thou do it for nothing else,   30 I am content.' So the master forgave him his saying, although he had said truth peradventure.

A.45: *Of the seruaunt that rymyd with hys mayster.*
B.47: *Of the seruant that rymyd with his master.*
D.26: *The seruant that rimed, &c.*

quickest: sharpest, liveliest (3).

sadly: soberly, solemnly (4, 6).

forsooth: indeed, certainly (28).

peradventure: perhaps (32).

Swapping rhymes would have been a common enough pastime in the sixteenth century. In his *Fool upon Fool* (1600), Robert Armin noted among the talents for which Henry VIII valued his fool Will Somers that:
    When he was sad, the king and he could rhyme—
    Thus, Will exiled sadness many a time.

48. Of the Welshman that delivered the letter to the ape.

A KNIGHT in Middlesex had a servant which had committed a felony whereof he was indicted, and because the term drew nigh, he feared he should be shortly arraigned thereof and in jeopardy of his life. Wherefore in all haste he sent a letter by a Welshman, a servant of his, unto the King's Justice of the King's Bench, requiring him to owe his lawful favour to his servant, and commanded his servant shortly to bring him an answer.

This Welshman came to the Chief Justice's place, and at the gate saw an ape sitting there in a coat made for him, as they use to apparel apes for disport.

This Welshman did off his cap and made courtesy to the ape and said, 'My master recommendeth him to my lord your father, and sendeth him here a letter.'

This ape took this letter and opened it and looked thereon, and after looked upon the man, making many mocks and mows as the property of apes is to do.

This Welshman, because he understood him not, came again to his master according to his commandment and said he had delivered the letter unto My Lord Chief Justice's son, which sat at the gate in a furred coat.

Anon, his master asked him what answer he had, which said he gave him an answer but it was either French or Latin for he understood him not.

'But, sir,' quod he, 'ye need not to fear, for I saw by his 25
countenance so much that I warrant you he will do your
errand surely to my lord his father.'

This gentleman in trust thereof made none other
labour, for lack whereof, his servant that had done the
felony within two days after was arraigned at the King's 30
Bench and cast, and afterward hanged.

*By this ye may see that every wise man ought to take heed
that he send no foolish servant upon a hasty message that is a
matter of weight.*

A.46: *Of the Welcheman that delyuered the letter to the ape.*
B.48: *Of the welchman that delyueryd the letter to the ape.*

Middlesex: the historic county of Middlesex was absorbed by Greater London in 1965 (1).

felony: a serious crime (2).

term: one of the four law terms, when all legal business was conducted (3).

shortly: swiftly, hastily (4, 8).

King's Bench: the court of law with jurisdiction over Middlesex (6).

disport: amusement, fun (11).

did off: took off (12).

made courtesy: bowed (12).

mocks and mows: jeers and grimaces (17).

property: nature, characteristic behaviour (17).

anon: soon, presently, shortly (22).

cast: sentenced (31).

from *Summa Praedicantium* by John of Bromyard (d.1352).

49.   Of him that sold right nought.

A CERTAIN fellow there was which proffered a dagger to sell to a fellow of his, which answered him and said that he had right nought to give him therefore.

Wherefore the other said that he should have his dagger upon condition that he should give and deliver unto him therefore within six days after, right nought or else forty shillings in money, whereto this other was content.

This bargain thus agreed, he that should deliver this right nought took no thought until such time that the day appointed drew nigh. At the which time, he began to imagine how he might deliver this man right nought. And first of all, he thought on a feather, a straw, a pin's point and such other. But nothing could he devise but that it was somewhat, wherefore he come home all sad and pensive for sorrow of losing of his forty shillings, and could neither sleep nor take rest. Whereof his wife, being aggrieved, demanded the cause of his heaviness. Which, at the last after many denies, told her all.

'Well, sir,' quod she, 'let me herewith alone, and get ye forth a-town, and I shall handle this matter well enough.'

This man, following his wife's counsel, went forth of the town and let his wife shift.

This woman then hung up an earthen pot, whereof the bottom was out, upon the wall by a cord. And when this other man come and asked for the good man, she said that he was not within.

182

'But, sir,' quod she, 'I know your errand well enough, for I wot well ye would have of mine husband forty shillings, because he cannot deliver to you this day right nought. Therefore, sir,' quod she, 'put your hand into yonder pot and take your money.'

This man, being glad, thrust his hand in it, supposing to have taken forty shillings of money, and thrust his hand through it up to the elbow.

Quod the wife then, 'Sir, what have ye there?'

'Marry,' quod he, 'right nought.'

'Sir,' quod she, 'then have ye your bargain, and then my husband hath contented you for his dagger according to his promise.'

By this ye may see that oftentimes a woman's wit at an extremity is much better than a man's.

A.47: *Of hym that solde ryght nought.*
B.49: *Of hym that sold ryght nought.*
D.29: *Of him that sauld richt nocht.*

right nought: absolutely nothing (3, *et al.*).

forty shillings: the equivalent of about £1,000 today (4-5, *et al.*).

somewhat: something (14).

herewith: with this (19).

a-town: to town (20).

shift: plan, work things out (22).

earthen: earthenware, pottery (23).

the bottom was out: the bottom of the pot had come away leaving a wide hole (23-4).

wot: know (28).

marry: indeed, certainly (36).

The moral is one of several concerned with the nature and status of women, *cf.* Tales 3, 10, 11, 19, 23, 29, 35, 46, 58, 66 and 97.

50. Of the friar that told the three children's fortunes.

THERE was a certain limiter which went a-limiting to a certain village, wherein dwelled a certain rich man of whom he never could get the value of an halfpenny, yet he thought he would go thither again to assay them. And as he went thitherward, the wife, standing at the door perceiving him coming afar off, thought that he would come thither and, by and by, ran in and bade her children standing at the door that if the friar asked for her, say she was not within. The friar saw her run in and suspected the cause, and came to the door and asked for the wife. The children, as they were bidden, said that she was not within.

Then stood he still, looking on the children and, at the last, he called to him the eldest and bade him let him see his hand. And, when he had seen his hand, 'O Jesu,' quod he, 'what fortune for thee is ordained!'

Then called he the second son to see his hand. And his hand seen, the friar said, 'O Lord, what a destiny for thee is prepared!'

Then looked he in the third son's hand. 'Surely,' quod he, 'thy destiny is hardest of all!'

And therewith went he his way.

The wife, hearing these things, suddenly ran out and called the friar again, and first made him to come in, and after to sit down, and set before him the best meat that she had, and when he had well eaten and drunken, she besought him to tell her the destinies of her children. Which, at the last after many denies, told her that the first should be a beggar, the second a thief, the third an homicide, which she hearing fell down in a swoon and took it grievously.

The friar comforted her and said that though these were their fortune, yet there might be remedy had. Then she besought him of his counsel.

Then said the friar, 'Ye must make the eldest that shall be a beggar, a friar; and the second that shall be a thief, a man of law; and the third that shall be an homicide, a physician.

By this tale ye may learn that they that will come to the speech or presence of any person for their own cause, they must first endeavour themself to show such matters as those persons most delight in.

limiter: a friar who paid his convent a fee for the exclusive right to beg within the limits of a fixed district (1).

limiting: begging within his prescribed limits (1).

halfpenny: a silver coin worth half a penny (½d.) the equivalent of about £1 today (3).

assay: try, test, attempt (4).

bade him let him see his hand: palmistry, or chiromancy, was forbidden by the Church but, for ordinary people, there was sometimes a thin line between religion and magic (14-5).

suddenly: immediately (23).

homicide: a murderer (30, 37).

physician: a doctor (38).

188

51. Of the boy that bore the friar his master's money.

A CERTAIN friar had a boy that ever was wont to bear this friar's money, and on a time when the boy was far behind his master as they two walked together by the way, there met a man the friar which knew that the boy bore the friars money and said, 'How, Master Friar! Shall I bid thy boy hie him apace after thee?'

'Yea,' quod the friar.

Then went the man to the boy and said, 'Sir, thy master biddeth thee give me forty pence.'

'I will not,' quod the boy.

Then called the man with a high voice to the friar and said, 'Sir, he saith he will not.'

Then quod the friar, 'Beat him!'

And when the boy heard his master say so, he gave the man forty pence.

By this ye may see it is folly for a man to say 'yea' or 'nay' to a matter, except he know surely what the matter is.

A.49: *Of the boy that bare the frere his masters money.*
B.51: *Of the boy that bare the frere hys masters money.*
D.30: *The boy that bare the, &c.*

hie: hasten (6).

apace: quickly (6).

forty pence: the equivalent of about £85 today (9).

a high voice: a loud voice (11).

The moral of this and the following tale warn against jumping to a hasty conclusion, see also Tale 85.

52.   Of Philip Spencer,
the butcher's man.

A CERTAIN butcher dwelling in St Nicholas Fleshambles in London, called Paul, had a servant called Peter. This Peter on a Sunday was at the church hearing Mass, and one of his fellows whose name was
5 Philip Spencer was sent to call him at the commandment of his master. So it happened at the time that the curate preached, and in his sermon touched many authorities of the Holy Scripture, among all, the words of the Epistle of St Paul *ad Philippenses*, that we be not only bound to
10 believe in Christ but also to suffer for Christ's sake, and said these words in the pulpit:

'What saith Paul *ad Philippenses* to this?'

This young man that was called Philip Spencer had weened he had spoken of him, answered shortly and said,
15 'Marry, sir, he bade Peter come home and take his part of a pudding, for he should go for a calf anon.'

The curate hearing this was abashed, and all the audience made great laughter.

By this tale ye may learn that it is no token of a wise man to
20 *give a sudden answer to a question, before that he know surely what the matter is.*

in St Nicholas Fleshambles: in the parish of St Nicholas Fleshambles; the church, which stood on the corner of Newgate Street and King Edward Street (formerly Butcher Hall Lane), was demolished in 1547 (1-2).

Fleshambles: the Shambles or Fleshambles were the butchers' shops which stood on the western part of Newgate Street (2).

fellows: associates, companions, co-workers (4).

curate: a priest charged with the cure or care of souls, a parish priest (6, 17).

Paul ad Philippenses: the Epistle of Paul and Timothy to the Philippians—*Epistola ad Philippenses* (9, 12).

weened: supposed, imagined (14).

shortly: promptly, swiftly (14).

marry: indeed, certainly (15).

take his part of a pudding: do his share in making (or eating) black pudding (15-6).

go for a calf: fetch a calf for slaughter (16).

anon: soon, presently, shortly (16).

abashed: disconcerted, embarrassed (17).

The moral of this and the preceding tale warn against jumping to a hasty conclusion, see also Tale 85.

53.   Of the courtier and the carter.

THERE came a courtier by a carter, the which in
derision praised the carter's back, legs and other
members of his body marvellously, whose jesting the
carter perceived and said he had another property than
5   the courtier espied in him. And when the courtier had
demanded what it should be, he looked aside over his
shoulder upon the courtier and said thus:

'Lo, sir, this is my property. I have a wall eye in my head,
for I never look over my shoulder this wise, but I lightly
10   espy a knave.'

*By this tale a man may see that he that useth to deride and
mock other folks is sometime himself more derided and
mocked.*

A.51: *Of the courtear and the carter.*
B.53: *Of the courtear and the carter.*
D.31: *The courteour & the carter.*

property: characteristic, attribute (4, 8).

wall eye: an eye that looks in another direction to the gaze (8).

lightly: readily, swiftly, usually (9).

The moral is among those which warn that treating others with scorn and derision can sometimes backfire, *cf.* Tales 2, 14, 60, 77 and 82.

A similar tale in the *Jests of Scoggin* (1565-6) tells 'How Scoggin told those that mocked him, that he had a wall eye':

Scoggin went up and down in the king's hall, and his hosen hung down, and his coat stood awry, and his hat stood 'a bonjour,' so every man did mock Scoggin. Some said he was a proper man, and did wear his raiment cleanly. Some said the whoreson fool could not put on his own raiment. Some said one thing, and some said another. At last Scoggin said, 'Masters, you have praised me well, but you did not espy one thing in me.'

'What is that, Tom?' said the men.

'Marry,' said Scoggin, 'I have a wall eye.'

'What meanest thou by that?' said the men.

'Marry,' said Scoggin, 'I have spied a sort of knaves that do mock me, and are worse fools themselves!'

54. Of the young man that prayed his fellow to teach him his Pater Noster.

A YOUNG man of the age of twenty year, rude and unlearned, in the time of Lent came to his curate to be confessed, which when he was of his life searched and examined, could not say his Pater Noster. Wherefore his confessor exhorted him to learn his Pater Noster, and showed him what an holy and goodly prayer it was and the effect thereof, and the seven petitions therein contained:

'The first petition beginneth, *Pater noster etc.* that is to say, "O Father, hallowed be Thy name, among men in Earth as among angels in Heaven."

'The second, *Adveniat etc.* "Let Thy kingdom come, and reign Thou among us men in Earth as among angels in Heaven."

'The third, *Fiat etc.* "Make us to fulfil Thy will here in Earth, as Thy angels in Heaven."

'The fourth, *Panem nostrum etc.* "Give us our daily sustenance alway and help us, as we give and help them that have need of us."

'The fifth, *Dimitte etc.* "Forgive us our sins done to Thee, as we forgive them that trespass against us."

'The sixth, *Et ne nos,* "Let us not be overcome with evil temptation."

'The seventh, *Sed libera etc.* "But deliver us from all evil. Amen."'

196

And then his confessor, after this exposition to him made, enjoined him in penance to fast every Friday, bread and water, till he had his Pater Noster well and sufficiently learned.

This young man meekly accepting his penance so departed and came home to one of his companions and said to his fellow, 'So it is, that my ghostly father hath given me in penance to fast every Friday, bread and water, till I can say my Pater Noster. Therefore, I pray thee, teach me my Pater Noster, and by my troth, I shall therefore teach thee a song of Robin Hood that shall be worth twenty of it!'

By this tale ye may learn to know the effect of the holy prayer of the Pater Noster.

A.52: *Of the yong man that prayd his felow to teche hym hys paternoster.*
B.54: *Of the yonge man that prayd his felow to tech hym his pater noster.*

Pater Noster: the Lord's Prayer, beginning in Latin with the words *Pater noster*, 'Our Father' (4, *et al.*).

rude: uneducated, uncouth (1).

curate: a priest charged with the cure or care of souls, a parish priest (2).

Pater noster etc.: Pater noster qui es in caelis, sanctificetur nomen tuum (8).

Adveniat etc.: Adveniat regnum tuum (11).

Fiat etc.: Fiat voluntas tua, sicut in caelo et in terra (14).

Panem nostrum etc.: Panem nostrum quotidianum da nobis hodie (16).

Dimitte etc.: Dimitte nobis debita nostra sicut et nos dimittimus debitoribus nostris (19).

Et ne nos: Et ne nos inducas in tentationem (21).

Sed libera etc.: Sed libera nos a malo. Amen (23).

ghostly: spiritual (31).

Robin Hood: tales of Robin Hood, which celebrated the values of the common man, appear to have been a byword among sophisticated Englishmen for the banal, the commonplace and the worthless (35).

In Rastell's *Interlude of the Four Elements* (1519), the character of Ignorance derides church music before saying:

> But if thou wilt have a song that is good,
> I have one of Robin Hood,
> The best that ever was made.

He then proceeds to sing a rambling sequence of unconnected, unrhymed lines, apparently drawing on stock phrases from the Robin Hood repertoire.

An anonymous poem of 1533-4, *The Image of Ipocrysy* (Part III), makes a similar point to this jest:

> Away these Bibles,
> For they be but riddles!
> And give them Robin Hood,
> To read how he stood
> In merry green wood,
> When he gathered good,
> Before Noah's Flood!

55. Of the friar that preached in rhyme expounding the Ave Maria.

A CERTAIN friar there was which upon Our Lady Day the Annunciation, made a sermon in the Whitefriars in London, and began his antetheme this wise: *Ave Maria, gratia plena, Dominus tecum etc.*

'These words,' quod the friar, 'were spoken by the Angel Gabriel to Our Lady when she conceived Christ, which is as much to say in our mother tongue as:

'All hail Mary, well thou be,

'The Son of God is with thee.

'And furthermore the angel said:

'Thou shalt conceive and bear a Son,

'And thou shalt call his name Jesum,

'And Elizabeth, thy sweet cousin,

'She shall conceive the sweet St John.'

And so proceeded still in his sermon in such fond rhyme that diverse and many gentlemen of the court that were there began to smile and laugh.

The friar that perceiving, said thus: 'Masters, I pray you hark! I shall tell you a narration:

'There was once a young priest that was not all the best clerk, said Mass and read a Collect thus: *Deus qui viginti filii tui etc.* wherefore he should have said *unigeniti filii tui etc.*

'And after, when Mass was done, there was such a gentleman as one of you are now, that had heard this Mass, came to the priest and said thus: "Sir, I pray you tell me, how many Sons had God Almighty?"

'Quod the priest, "Why ask you that?"

'"Marry, sir," quod the gentleman, "I suppose he had twenty Sons, for ye said right now, *Deus qui viginti filii tui.*"

'The priest perceiving how that he derided him, answered him shortly and said thus: "How many Sons so ever God Almighty had, I am sure that thou art none of them, for thou scornest the Word of God."

'And so,' said the friar in the pulpit, 'no more are ye none of the children of God, for ye scorn and laugh at me now that preach to you the Word of God.'

Which words made the gentlemen and all the other people laugh much more than they did before.

By this tale a man may learn to perceive well that the best the wisest and the most holiest matter that is, by fond pronunciation and utterance may be marred, nor shall not edify to the audience. Therefore, every process would be uttered with words and countenance convenient to the matter.

Also yet by this tale, they that be unlearned in the Latin tongue may know the sentence of the Ave Maria.

A.53: Of the frere that prechyd in ryme expownynge the ave maria.
B.55: Of the frere that prechyd in ryme expownyng the aue maria

Ave Maria: Hail Mary—the opening words of the prayer Ave Maria are based on the Biblical text of Luke 1:28 (*Et ingressus angelus ad eam dixit, Ave gratia plena, Dominus tecum, benedicta tu in mulieribus*), which is the subject of the friar's sermon (4).

Whitefriars: the Carmelite friary stood to the south of Fleet Street between Temple and Whitefriars Street; Carmelites were known as White Friars because of the white cloaks they wore (3).

antetheme: an introduction to the text of a sermon, preceding the main discussion of the theme (3).

Jesum: Jesus, reflecting the case ending in the Latin of Luke 1:31, *et vocabis nomen ejus Jesum* (12).

fond: foolish, silly (15, 41).

clerk: a cleric, a scholar (21).

Collect: a formal, structured prayer forming part of the liturgy of the Mass (21).

Deus qui viginti filii tui: 'God who of your twenty son(s) ...' (21-2, 30).

unigeniti filii tui: 'of your only begotten Son' —the letters 'u' and 'v' were frequently treated as interchangeable (23).

marry: indeed, certainly (29).

shortly: promptly, briskly (32).

convenient: suitable, appropriate (44).

sentence: teaching, authority (46).

The second part of this tale reappears in the *Jests of Scoggin* (1565-6) where it is told of the Parson of Baldon, Oxfordshire:

On a time, Master Scoggin said to his fellows that were Masters of Art, 'I pray you, let us go to make merry with the Parson of Baldon, which was once my scholar.'

'Be it,' said they.

On the morrow in the morning, they went to Baldon, and one Master of Art went before all the other, and did go into the church, and the priest began Mass of the Cross, and when he came to the Collect he did read, '*Deus qui viginti filii tui, etc.*' when he should have said, '*Deus qui unigeniti, etc.*' And as he was reading the Collect, he heard a great noise in the churchyard, and ere he had fully made an end of it, Master Scoggin and the other Masters of Art came into the church. Then at the Collect end, he turned about and said, '*Dominus, vobiscum.*' He, spying so many scholars, said, '*Ite missa est,*' for he thought the scholars did come for to check him in his Mass.

And when Mass was done, they went to dinner with the parson. And after dinner, the Master of Art that did come first into the church, that heard the parson read, *Deus qui viginti filii tui*, said, 'Master Parson, I pray you for my learning, tell me how many sons God had.'

The Parson was astonished. 'Sir,' said he, 'I will tell you by and by.'

He went to Scoggin saying, 'Sir, I pray you tell me how many sons God had.'

Scoggin said, 'Go and tell him, "Sir, you did ask of me how many sons God hath. It shall not skill how many nor how few he hath, I am sure that you be none of them!"'

'Why, sir,' said the Master of Art, 'you said today in your Mass, that God had twenty children, for you said, *Deus qui viginti filii tui.*'

'Yea sir, be content,' said Scoggin. 'Hath God mo or less, my priest saith you be none of them. We have good cheer, and costs us nothing. Therefore, one good turn asketh another without reprehension.'

56. Of the curate that preached the Articles of the Creed.

IN a village in Warwickshire there was a parish priest, and though he were no great clerk nor graduate of the university, yet he preached to his parishioners upon a Sunday, declaring to them the Twelve Articles of the Creed,
5 showing them that: the First Article was to believe in God the Father, Almighty Maker of Heaven and Earth; the Second, to believe in Jesu Christ, his only Son, Our Lord, coequal with the Father in all things pertaining to the Deity; the Third, that He was conceived of the Holy Ghost,
10 born of the Virgin Mary; the Fourth, that He suffered death under Pontius Pilate, and that He was crucified dead and buried; the Fifth, that He descended to Hell and fetched out the good souls that were in Faith and Hope, and that He the third day rose from death to life; the Sixth,
15 He ascended into Heaven to the right side of God the Father, where He sitteth; the Seventh, that He shall come at the Day of Doom to Judge both us that be quick and them that be dead; the Eighth, to believe in the Holy Ghost, equal God with the Father and the Son; the Ninth,
20 in the Holy Church Catholic, and in the Holy Communion of Saints; the Tenth, in the Remission of Sins; the Eleventh, in the Resurrection General of the body and soul; the Twelfth, in Everlasting Life that God shall reward them that be good.

And said to his parishioners further that these articles, 25
'ye be bound to believe, for they be true and of authority.
And if you believe not me, then for a more surety and
sufficient authority, go your way to Coventry, and there ye
shall see them all played in Corpus Christi Play.'

By reading of this tale they they that understand no Latin may 30
learn to know the Twelve Articles of the Faith.

A.54: *Of the curat that prechyd the Artycles of the Crede.*
B.56: *Of the curat that prechyd the artycles of the Crede.*

curate: a priest charged with the cure or care of souls, a parish priest.

Articles: the text of the Apostles' Creed (a conventional Christian statement of faith)
consists of twelve 'Articles' or specific points of belief (4, *et al.*).

clerk: a cleric, a scholar (2).

quick: living, alive (17).

Resurrection General: the universal resurrection which, according to Christian teaching,
precedes the Last Judgment (22).

Corpus Christi Play: at Coventry the Mystery Plays were performed at the feast of Corpus
Christi in early summer. The priest refers his listeners to the Corpus Christi Play as if
it has the weight of genuine religious Authority (29).

Although a sixteenth-century text survives for the Coventry Corpus Christi plays, they
had apparently been rewritten in 1519, whereas Rastell's story was probably current
before he left Coventry in 1508. Neither of the two plays which survives from Coventry
includes a passage on the Articles of the Creed, but the *Chester Pentecost Play* does include
appropriate verses (lines 311-58) and the equivalent passage in the earlier Coventry
plays may have been similar.

57. Of the friar that preached the Ten Commandments.

A LIMITER of the Greyfriars in London, which preached in a certain village in the country in the time of his limitation, and had but one sermon which he had learned by heart that was of the declaring of the Ten Commandments:

The first, to believe in one God, and to honour Him above all thing.

The second, to swear not in vain by Him nor none other of His creatures.

The third, to abstain from worldly operation on the Holy Day, thou and all thy servants of whom thou hast charge.

The fourth, to honour thy parents and to help them in their necessity.

The fifth, to slay no man in deed nor will, nor for no hatred hurt his body nor good name.

The sixth, to do no fornication actual, nor by no unleeful thought to desire no fleshly delectation.

The seventh, to steal nor deprive no man's goods by theft, robbery, extortion, usury, nor deceit.

The eighth, to bear no false witness to hurt another, nor to tell no lies, nor to say nothing against truth.

The ninth, to covet nor desire no man's goods unleefully.

The tenth, to covet nor to desire thy neighbour's wife for thine own appetite unleefully.

And because this friar had preached this sermon so often, one that had heard it before told the friar's servant that his master was called 'Friar John Ten Commandments,' wherefore this servant showed the friar his master thereof and advised him to preach some sermon of some other matter, for it grieved him to hear his master so derided and to be called Friar John Ten Commandments, 'for every man knoweth what ye will say as soon as ever ye begin, because ye have preached it so oft.'

'Why then,' quod the friar, 'I am sure thou knowest well which be the Ten Commandments, that hast heard them so oft declared.'

'Yea, sir,' quod the servant, 'that I do.'

Then quod the friar, 'I pray thee, rehearse them unto me now.'

'Marry,' quod the servant, 'these be they: Pride; Covetousness; Sloth; Envy; Wrath; Gluttony; and Lechery.'

By reading this tale ye may learn to know the Ten Commandments and the Seven Deadly Sins.

A.55: *Of the frere that prechyd the x commaundementis.*
B.57: *Of the frere that prechyd the .x. comaundmentys.*

limiter: a friar who paid his convent a fee for the exclusive right to beg within the limits of a fixed district (1).

Greyfriars: the monastery of the Franciscans or 'Grey Friars' (so called because of their grey habit) once stood near Newgate; after its dissolution in 1538, Greyfriars became a parish church, but the medieval building was destroyed in the Great Fire of 1666, and its replacement was destroyed in 1940 during the Blitz (1).

time of his limitation: the duration of his tenure as a limiter (3).

unleeful; unleefully: unpermitted, unlawful; unlawfully (18; 24, 26).

servant: friars' servants seem typically to have been boys, for whom their service might have formed part of their wider education—*cf.* Tales 33, 36, 37, and 51 (29, *et al.*).

marry: indeed, certainly (43).

Seven Deadly Sins: listed here (lines 43-4) as Pride, Covetousness (Greed), Sloth (Idleness or Apathy), Envy, Wrath (Anger), Gluttony, and Lechery (Lust) (46).

58.   Of the wife that bade her husband eat the candle first.

THE husband said to his wife thus wise: 'By this candle, I dreamed this night that I was a cuckold!'

To whom she answered and said, 'Husband, by this bread, ye are none!'

Then said he, 'Wife, eat the bread.'

She answered and said to her husband, 'Then eat you the candle, for you swore first.'

By this a man may see that a woman's answer is never to seek.

A.56: *Of the wyfe that bad her husbande ete the candell fyrste.*
B.58: *Of the wyfe that bad her husband ete the candell furst.*
D.27: *The wife that bade hir &c.*

by this candle: the understanding is that the candle will turn against him if the husband has perjured himself, so it might be expected to sputter or die, if he has sworn falsely (1-2).

cuckold: a man with an unfaithful wife (2).

by this bread: as with the husband's oath by the candle, the understanding is that the bread will turn against the wife if she has perjured herself, and so might cause stomach ache or be difficult to swallow, if she tries to eat it (3-4).

eat you the candle: this is probably a tallow candle made from rendered animal fat, but still barely more palatable than one made from beeswax (6-7).

a woman's answer is never to seek: i.e. a woman has a ready answer for anything so there is no need to go looking for it, with a secondary meaning that it is not to be looked for because it won't be what you want to hear—*cf.* Tale 23 'Of the maid washing clothes that answered the friar' and Tale 29 'Of the gentleman that wished his tooth in the gentlewoman's tail' (8).

The moral is one of several concerned with the nature and status of women, *cf.* Tales 3, 10, 11, 19, 23, 29, 35, 46, 49, 66 and 97.

59.   Of the man of law's son's answer.

A WOMAN demanded a question of a young child,
son unto a man of law, of what craft his father was.
Which child said his father was 'a crafty man of law.'

By this tale a man may perceive that sometime peradventure
5   *young innocents speak truly unadvised.*

A.57: *Of the man of lawes sonnes answer.*
B.59: *Of the man of lawys sonnys answer.*
D.28: *Of the woman that, &c.*

craft: a profession, a trade (2).

crafty: learned, intelligent, skilled in a craft, sly, cunning, deceitful; the usual modern sense of the word is most important here, but the child intends it to mean that his father is learned in the craft of law (3).

peradventure: perhaps (4).

speak truly unadvised: to speak truth without knowledge; for a similar moral, *cf.* Tale 87 (5).

60. Of the friar in the pulpit that bade the woman leave her babbling.

IN a certain parish church in London, after the old laudable and accustomed manner, there was a friar minor. Although he were not the best clerk, nor could not make the best sermons, yet by the licence of the curate he there preached to the parishioners.

Among the which audience there was a wife, at that time little disposed to contemplation, talked with a gossip of hers of other feminine tales so loud that the friar heard and somewhat was perturbed therewith. To whom therefore openly the friar spoke and said, 'Thou woman there in the tawny gown, hold thy peace and leave thy babbling! Thou troublest the Word of God.'

This woman, therewith suddenly abashed because the friar spoke to her so openly that all the people her beheld, answered shortly and said, 'I beshrew his heart that babbled more of us two.'

At the which saying, the people did laugh because they felt but little fruit in his sermon.

By this tale a man may learn to beware how he openly rebuketh any other and in what audience, lest it turn to his own reproof.

A.58: *Of the frere in the pulpet that bad the woman leve her babelynge.*
B.60: *Of the frere in the pulpit that bad the woman leue her babelyng.*
D.32: *The freir in the pulpit, &c.*

friar minor: a Franciscan friar belonging to the Order of Friars Minor—Latin, *Fratres Minores* (2-3).

clerk: a cleric, a scholar (3).

curate: a priest charged with the cure or care of souls, a parish priest (4).

gossip: a godparent or godchild, a close friend or companion (7).

tawny: a brownish shade, fashionable in dyed clothes for all ranks (11).

suddenly: instantly, immediately (13).

abashed: became disconcerted or embarrassed (13).

shortly: briskly, hastily (15).

beshrew: to curse (15).

The moral is among those which warn that treating others with scorn and derision can sometimes backfire, *cf.* Tales 2, 14, 53, 77 and 82.

61.   Of the Welshman that cast the Scot into the sea.

IN the reign of the most mighty and victorious prince, King Henry the Eighth, cruel war began between Englishmen, Frenchmen and Scots. The Englishmen were so mighty upon the sea, that none other people of other realms were able to resist them, wherefore they took many great enterprises and many ships, and many prisoners of other realms that were their enemies. Among the which they happened on a season to take a Scottish ship, and diverse Scots they slew and took prisoners.

Among whom there was a Welshman that had one of the Scots prisoner, and bade him that he should do off his harness, which to do the Scot was very loath. Howbeit, for fear at the last he pulled it off with an ill will, and said to the Welshman, 'If thou wilt needs have my harness, take it there!' and cast it over the board into the sea.

The Welshman seeing that said, 'By Cot's Plut and Her Nail, I shall make her fetch it again,' and took him by the legs and cast him after over the board into the sea.

By this tale a man may learn that he that is subject to another ought to forsake his own will, and follow his will and commandment that so hath subjection over him, lest it turn to his greater hurt and damage.

cruel war: Henry VIII campaigned successfully against France in 1512-3, and James IV of Scotland led a disastrous counter-attack on England in support of the French; Rastell was employed in an organisational capacity in the campaign in France (2).

do off: take off (11).

harness: armour (12).

Cot's Plut and Her Nail: God's Blood and His [Crucifixion] Nail—in imitation of the Welshman's accent (16-7).

make her fetch it: make him fetch it—in imtation of the Welshman's accent (17).

The moral may be compared with that for Tale 13.

62.   Of the man that had the dumb wife.

THERE was a man that married a woman which had great riches and beauty, howbeit she had such an impediment of nature that she was dumb and could not speak, which thing made him full oft to be right pensive and sad.

Wherefore upon a day as he walked alone right heavy in heart thinking upon his wife, there came one to him and asked him what was the cause of his heaviness. Which answered that it was only because his wife was born dumb.

To whom this other said, 'I shall show thee soon a remedy and a medicine therefore, that is thus: Go take an aspen leaf and lay it under her tongue this night, she being asleep, and I warrant thee that she shall speak on the morrow.'

Which man, being glad of this medicine, prepared therefore and gathered aspen leaves. Wherefore, he laid three of them under her tongue when she was asleep.

And upon the morrow when he himself waked, he, desirous to know how his medicine wrought, being in bed with her, demanded of her how she did, and suddenly she answered and said, 'I beshrew your heart for waking me so early!' and so by virtue of that medicine she was restored to her speech.

But in conclusion, her speech so increased day by day 25
and she was so cursed of condition, that every day she
brawled and chid with her husband so much, that at the
last he was more vexed and had much more trouble and
disease with her shrewd words than he had before when
she was dumb. 30

Wherefore, as he walked another time alone, he
happened to meet again with the same person that taught
him the said medicine, and said to him this wise:

'Sir, ye taught me a medicine but late to make my dumb
wife to speak, bidding me lay an aspen leaf under her 35
tongue when she slept. And I laid three aspen leaves there,
wherefore now she speaketh. But yet she speaketh so
much and so shrewdly, that I am more weary of her now
than I was before when she was dumb. Wherefore, I pray
you, teach me a medicine to modify her, that she speak 40
not so much.'

This other answered and said thus:

'Sir, I am a devil of Hell, but I am one of them that have
least power there. Albeit yet I have power to make a
woman to speak, but yet if a woman begin once to speak, 45
I nor all the devils in Hell that have the most power be not
able to make a woman to be still, nor to cause her to leave
her speaking.'

By this tale ye may note that a man oft times desireth and
coveteth too much that thing that oft turneth to his displeasure. 50

A.60: *Of the man that had the dome wyfe.*
B.62: *Of the man that had the dome wyfe.*
D.33: *The man that had the dum, &c.*

dumb: mute, unable to speak (3, *et al.*).

aspen leaf: aspen leaves quiver or tremble in the breeze with a distinctive whispering sound—cf. Tale 19 'Of the four Elements, where they should soon be found' (13, *et al.*).

suddenly: abruptly, immediately (21).

beshrew: to curse (22).

brawled: quarrelled, spoke loudly (27).

disease: lack of ease, trouble (29).

shrewd: shrewish, scolding (29).

wise: manner, way (33).

shrewdly: shrewishly, scoldingly (38).

The moral is one of several concerned with covetousness, miserliness, and attitudes to money and personal possessions, cf. Tales 15, 17, 20, 33, 68, 78, 90, 91 and 100.

The same story is retold in verse in *The Schoolhouse of Women* (c.1541):

> Another reason, if ye mark well,
> Doth cause the woman of words be rife:
> A certain man, as fortune fell,
> A woman tongueless wedded to wife,
> Whose frowning countenance perceiving, be lieve
> Till he might know what men thought long,
> And wished full oft she had a tongue.
>
> The devil was ready, and appeared anon.
> An aspen leaf he bade the man take,
> And in her mouth should put but one.
> 'A tongue,' said the devil, 'it shall her make.'
> Till he had done, his head did ache—
> Leaves he gathered, and took plenty,
> And in her mouth put two or three.

Within a while, this medicine wrought.
The man could tarry no longer time,
But wakened her, to the end he mought
The virtue prove of the medicine.
The first word she spake to him,
She said, 'Thou whoreson, knave, and thief,
How durst thou waken me with a mischief!'

From that day forward, she never ceased;
Her boister-babble grieved him sore.
The devil he met, and him entreated
To make her tongueless, as she was before.
'Not so,' said the devil, 'I will meddle no more!
One devil a woman to speak may constrain,
But all that in Hell be cannot let it again!'

And by proof, daily we see
What inclination Nature maketh:
The aspen leaf, hanging where it be,
With little wind or none, it shaketh;
A woman's tongue in like wise, taketh
Little ease and little rest
For, if it should, the heart would burst.

(lines 511-545)

Essentially the same story is also retold by Rabelais in his *Third Book of Pantagruel*, ch.34 (1546).

63. Of the Proctor of Arches
that had the little wife.

ONE asked a Proctor of the Arches, lately before married, why he chose him so little a wife.

Which answered, because he had a text saying thus:

Ex duobus malis, minus malum est eligendum—that is to say in English, 'Among evil things the least is to be chosen.'

A.61: *Of the Proctour of Arches that had the lytel wyfe.*
B.63: *Of the proctor of arches that had the lytell wyfe.*
D.34: *The proctor of Archies, &c.*

Proctor of Arches: a procurator or legal representative to the ecclesiastical Arches Court of Canterbury, which was held in the church of St Mary-le-Bow, London (1).

ex duobus malis minus malum est eligendum: 'out of two evils, the lesser evil is chosen'—a legal formula invoked in judgements (4).

This tale also appears in Ottmar Luscinius's *Joci ac Sales mire festivi* (Augsburg, 1524) where it is told of Aristotle. If Rastell changed the protagonist from Aristotle to an unnamed 'Proctor of Arches', he may have deliberately removed a Classical reference, but both writers were part of the same humanist circle which included Erasmus and Sir Thomas More, and the tale probably circulated orally before it was first written down.

223

64. Of the two nuns that were shriven of one priest.

IN the time of Lent, there came two nuns to St John's in London because of the Great Pardon, there to be confessed. Of the which nuns the one was a young lady and the other was old.

5   This young lady chose first her confessor, and confessed her that she had sinned in Lechery. The confessor asked with whom it was. She said it was with a lusty gallant.

He demanded where it was. She said in a pleasant, green arbour.

10   He asked further when it was. She said in the merry month of May.

Then said the confessor this wise:

'A fair young lady with a lusty gallant in a pleasant arbour and in the merry month of May! Ye did but your
15   kind. Now, by my troth, God forgive you and I do.'

And so she departed, and incontinent the old nun met with her, asking her how she liked her confessor. Which said that he was the best ghostly father that ever she had, and the most easiest in penance giving. For
20   comfort whereof, this other nun went to the same confessor and shrove her likewise that she had sinned in Lechery. And he demanded with whom, which said with an old friar.

He asked where. She said in her old cloister.
25   He asked what season. She said in Lent.

Then the confessor said thus:

'An old whore to lie with an old friar in her old cloister and in the holy time of Lent! By Cock's Body, if God forgive thee, yet will I never forgive thee.'

Which words caused her to depart all sad and sore abashed. 30

By this tale men may learn that a vicious act is more abominable in one person than in another, in one season than in another, and in one place than in another.

A.62: *Of ii nonnes that were shryuen of one preste.*
B.64: *Of the .ii. nonnys that were shryuyn of one prest.*

shriven: confessed, granted Absolution of sins through Confession.

Lent: Christian penitentials demanded sexual abstinence during Lent and Advent (1, *et al.*).

St John's: the Priory Church of St John of Jerusalem, Clerkenwell Priory, was the sole English outpost of the Knights Hospitaller; the chancel and crypt survive to this day, along with St John's Gate to the south, and the street name St John Street (1).

Great Pardon: in 1451 'came a legate from the Pope of Rome with great pardon, for that pardon was the greatest pardon that ever came to England from the Conquest unto this time' (Gregory's *Chronicle of London*, MS Egerton 1995, *cf.* Gairdner p.197) (2).

Lechery: one of the Seven Deadly Sins, for which see Tale 57 'Of the friar that preached the Ten Commandments' (6).

kind: nature (15).

incontinent: straight away, immediately (16).

ghostly: spiritual (18).

Cock's Body: a meaningless, non-blasphemous substitution for 'God's Body' (28).

abashed: perturbed, disconcerted (31).

65. Of the esquire that should have been made knight.

WHEN the most noble and fortunate prince, Edward of England, made war in France with great puissance and army of people, whom the French king with another great host encountered; and when both the hosts should join, and the trumpets began to blow, a young squire of England riding on a lusty courser, of which horse the noise of the trumpets so pricked the courage that the squire could not him retain, so that against his will he ran upon his enemies. Which squire, seeing none other remedy, set his spear in the rest and rode through the thickest of his enemies, and in conclusion had good fortune, and saved himself alive without hurt, and the English host followed and had the victory.

And after, when the field was done, this King Edward called the squire and bade him kneel down, for he would make him knight because that he valiantly was the man that day which, with the most courageous stomach, adventured first upon their enemies.

To whom the squire thus answered: 'If it like Your Grace to make anybody knight therefore, I beseech you to make my horse knight and not me, for certes, it was his deed and not mine, and full sore against my will.'

Which answer the king hearing, refrained to promote him to the order of knighthood, reputing him in manner but for a coward, and ever after favoured him the less therefore. 25

By this tale a man may learn how it is wisdom for one that is in good credence to keep him therein, and in no wise to disable himself too much.

A.63: *Of the esquyer that sholde haue ben made knight.*
B.65: *Of the esquyer that sholde haue bene made knyght.*
D.35: *The Esquyre that sould, &c.*

esquire: a gentleman entitled to bear arms.

puissance: power, force of arms (3).

certes: certainly (21).

disable: disparage, disqualify (29).

This tale probably refers not to Edward IV's brief and uneventful French campaign of 1475, but to the incessant wars of Edward III and his son, Edward the Black Prince, a hundred years before.

66. Of the man that would have the pot stand there as he would.

A YOUNG man late married to a wife, thought it was good policy to get the mastery of her in the beginning, came to her, the pot seething over the fire, although the meat therein were not enough, suddenly commanded her to take the pot from the fire. Which answered, and said that the meat was not ready to eat.

And he said again, 'I will have it taken off, for my pleasure.'

This good woman, loath yet to offend him, set the pot beside the fire as he bade. And anon after, he commanded her to set the pot behind the door, and she said thereto again, 'Ye be not wise therein.'

But he precisely said it should be so as he bade. And she gently again did his commandment.

This man, yet not satisfied, commanded her to set the pot a-high upon the hen roost.

'What!' quod the wife again, 'I trow ye be mad.'

And he fiercely then commanded her to set it there, or else he said she should repent it. She, somewhat afraid to move his patience, took a ladder and set it to the roost, and went herself up the ladder and took the pot in her hand, praying her husband then to hold the ladder fast for sliding, which so did.

And when the husband looked up and saw the pot stand there on height, he said thus:

'Lo! now standeth the pot there as I would have it.'

This wife hearing that, suddenly poured the hot potage on his head and said thus:

'And now been the potage there as I would have them.'

By this tale men may see it is no wisdom for a man to [30] *attempt a meek woman's patience too far, lest it turn to his own hurt and damage.*

A.64: *Of hym that wolde gette the maystrye of his wyfe.*
B.66: *Of the man that wold haue the pot stand there as he wold.*
D.36: *The woman that dyd, &c.*

seething: boiling (3).

enough: cooked, done—*cf.* Tale 92 (4).

anon: soon, presently, shortly (10).

a-high: on high (16).

trow: think, believe (17).

hold … fast: hold firmly, hold still (22).

suddenly: abruptly, immediately (27).

potage: stew, thick soup—treated as a plural (27, 29).

The moral is one of several concerned with the nature and status of women, *cf.* Tales 3, 10, 11, 19, 23, 29, 35, 46, 49, 58 and 97.

The same story is retold in verse in *The Schoolhouse of Women* (c.1541):

> Say what ye will, they will do as them list—
> The proof thereof in a certain fable:
> A husbandman, having good trust
> His wife to him had be agreeable,
> Thought to attempt if she had be reformable,
> Bade take the pot that sod [seethed] over the fire
> And set it above, upon the astire [hearth].
>
> She answered him, 'I hold thee mad
> And I more fool, by Saint Martin,
> The dinner is ready as thou me bade,
> And time it were that thou shouldest dine—
> And thou wilt not, I will go to mine.'
> 'I bid thee,' said he, 'bear up the pot.'
> 'Aha,' she said, 'I trow thou dote!'
>
> Up she goeth for fear at last,
> No question moved where it should stand,
> Upon his head the potage she cast
> And held the pot still in her hand,
> And towards him she cursed and banned,
> Said and swore he might her trust,
> She would with the potage do what her list!

(lines 623-643)

67. Of the penitent that said, 'The Sheep of God have mercy upon me.'

A CERTAIN confessor in the holy time of Lent enjoined his penitent to say daily for his penance this prayer: '*Agnus dei miserere mei*,' which was as much to say in English as, 'The Lamb of God have mercy upon me.'

5   This penitent accepting his penance, departed, and that time twelve month after, came again to be confessed of the same confessor, which demanded of him whether he had fulfilled his penance that he him enjoined the last year.

    And he said thus: 'Yea, sir, I thank God I have fulfilled
10 it, for I have said thus today in the morning and so daily: "The Sheep of God have mercy upon me."'

    To whom the confessor said, 'Nay, I bade thee say, *Agnus dei miserere mei*, that is, "The Lamb of God have mercy upon me."'

15   'Yea, sir,' quod the penitent, 'ye say truth. That was the last year, but now it is a twelvemonth sith, and it is a sheep by this time. Therefore I must needs say now, "The Sheep of God have mercy upon me."'

By this tale ye may perceive that if holy scripture be
20 *expounded to rude lay people only in the literal sense,*
peradventure it shall do but little good.

A.65: *Of the penytent that sayd the shepe of God haue mercy vpon me.*
B.67: *Of the penytent that sayd the shepe of god haue mercy vpon me.*

Lamb of God: i.e. Jesus (see John 1:29) —a reference to the traditional Jewish sacrificial lamb of Passover (4, 13).

twelvemonth: a year (16).

sith: since (16).

rude: uneducated, uncouth (20).

peradventure: perhaps (21).

The moral is among several which contrast wisdom, learning and orderly behaviour with foolishness, wilfulness and stupidity, *cf.* Tales 1, 5, 8, 34, 37, 69, 71, 73, 75 and 81.

A secular parallel to this tale is found in Tale 103, 'Of the man that painted the lamb upon his wife's belly.'

John Baptyſt.

68. Of the husband that said he was John Daw.

IT fortuned diverse to be in communication, among whom there was a curate or a parish priest and one John Daw, a parishioner of his, which two had communication more busy than other in this manner:

5   This priest thought that one might not by feeling know one from another in the dark.

John Daw his parishioner, of the contrary opinion, laid with his curate for a wager forty pence.

Whereupon the parish priest, willing to prove his 10 wager, went to this John Daw's house in the evening and suddenly got him to bed with his wife where, when he began to be somewhat busy, she, feeling his crown, said shortly with a loud voice, 'By God, thou art not John Daw!'

That hearing, her husband answered, 'Thou sayest 15 truth, wife. I am here John Daw. Therefore, Master Parson, give me the money, for ye have lost your forty pence.'

By this tale ye may learn to perceive that it is no wisdom for a man, for the covetise of winning of any wager, to put in jeopardy a thing that may turn him to greater displeasure.

A.66: *Of the husbande that sayd he was John daw.*
B.68: *Of the husband that sayd he was John daw.*

curate: a priest charged with the cure or care of souls, a parish priest (2, 8).

forty pence: the equivalent of about £85 today (8, 16).

prove: test, try (9).

suddenly: immediately, abruptly (11).

his crown: the crown of his head—the priest's crown is shaven in a tonsure (12).

shortly: quickly, promptly (13).

covetise: covetousness, greed (18).

The moral is one of several concerned with covetousness, miserliness, and attitudes to money and personal possessions, *cf.* Tales 15, 17, 20, 33, 62, 78, 90, 91 and 100.

69. Of the scholar of Oxford that proved by sophistry two chickens three.

A RICH franklin in the country, having by his wife but one child and no more, for the great affection that he had to his said child, found him at Oxford to school by the space of two or three year. This young scholar in a vacation time for his disport came home to his father.

It fortuned afterward on a night, the father, the mother and the said young scholar sitting at supper, having before them no more meat but only a couple of chickens, the father said this wise:

'Son, so it is that I have spent much money upon thee to find thee to school, wherefore I have great desire to know what thou hast learned.'

To whom the son answered and said, 'Father, I have studied sophistry and, by that science, I can prove that these two chickens in the dish be three chickens.'

'Marry,' said the father, 'that would I fain see.'

The scholar took one of the chickens in his hand and said, 'Lo! here is one chicken,' and incontinent he took both the chickens in his hand jointly and said, 'Here is two chickens. And one and two maketh three. *Ergo*, here is three chickens.'

Then the father took one of the chickens to himself and gave another to his wife, and said thus:

'Lo! I will have one of the chickens to my part, and thy mother shall have another, and because of thy good argument thou shalt have the third to thy supper, for thou gettest no more meat here at this time!'

Which promise the father kept, and so the scholar went without his supper.

By this tale men may see that it is great folly to put one to school to learn any subtle science which hath no natural wit.

A.67: *Of the scoler of Oxforde that proued by souestry ii chykens iii.*
B.69: *Of the skoler of oxford that prouyd by souphestry .ii. chickens .iii.*
D.37: *The scholer of Oxford, &c.*

sophistry: the deliberate use of fallacious reasoning in order to deceive (14).

franklin: a free landowner—one step down from a gentleman (1).

found: supported, maintained, funded (3).

disport: amusement, fun (5).

to find: to support, maintain, fund (11).

marry: indeed, certainly (16).

fain: gladly, wishfully, heartily (16).

incontinent: straight away, immediately (18).

ergo: therefore (Latin) (20).

The moral is among several which contrast wisdom, learning and orderly behaviour with foolishness, wilfulness and stupidity, *cf.* Tales 1, 5, 8, 34, 37, 67, 71, 73, 75 and 81.

Similar tales appear in Ottmar Luscinius's *Joci ac Sales mire festivi* (Augsburg, 1524) and the *Jests of Scoggin* (1565-6):

Scoggin on a time had two eggs to his breakfast, and Jack his scholar should roast them, and as they were roasting, Scoggin went to the fire to warm him, and as the eggs were roasting Jack said, 'Sir, I can by sophistry prove that here be three eggs.'

'Let me see that,' said Scoggin.

'I shall tell you, sir,' said Jack. 'Is not here one?'

'Yes,' said Scoggin.

'And is not here two?' said Jack.

'Yea,' said Scoggin, 'of that I am sure.'

Then Jack did tell the first egg again saying, 'Is not this the third?'

'Oh,' said Scoggin, 'Jack, thou art a good sophister. Well,' said Scoggin, 'these two eggs shall serve me for my breakfast, and take thou the third for thy labour, and for the herring that thou didst give me the last day.'

So, one good turn doth ask another, and to deceive him that goeth about to deceive is no deceit.

70. Of the friar that stole the pudding.

A FRIAR of London there was, that on a Sunday morning early in the summer season, came from London to Barnet to make a collation, and was there an hour before High Mass began and, because he would come to the church honestly, he went first to an alehouse there to wipe his shoes and to make himself cleanly. In the which house there were puddings to sell, and diverse folks there breaking their fast and eating puddings. But the friar broke his fast in a secret place in the same house.

This friar soon after came to the church and, by licence of the curate, entered into the pulpit to make a collation or sermon. And in his sermon there he rebuked sore the manner of them that used to break their fast on the Sunday before High Mass, and said it was called 'The Devil's Black Breakfast.' And with that word speaking, as he did cast his arms out to make his countenance, there fell a pudding out of his sleeve which he himself had stolen a little before in the same alehouse.

And when the people saw that, and specially they that broke their fast there the same morning and knew well that the wife had complained how she had one of her puddings stolen, they laughed so much at the friar that he incontinent went down out of the pulpit for shame.

By this tale a man may see that when a preacher doth rebuke any sin or vice wherein he is known openly to be guilty himself, such preaching shall little edify to the people.

A.68: *Of the frere that stale the podynge.*
B.70: *Of the frere that stale the podyng.*

Barnet: now a London Borough, Barnet was then in the county of Hertfordshire on the border with Middlesex; Rastell leased a country house in nearby Monken Hadley from 1515 (3).

collation: a homily or sermon (3, 11).

honestly: respectably, respectfully (5).

puddings: black puddings (7, *et al.*).

curate: a priest charged with the cure or care of souls, a parish priest (11).

countenance: a gesture, an expressive movement (15).

incontinent: straight away, immediately (23).

This story is retold in the anonymous *Tarlton's News out of Purgatory* (c.1590) where, perhaps because England was no longer Catholic, the action is transferred to Bergamo in Lombardy:

Every Sunday morning afore mass, all the youth of the parish did accustom to come to the alehouse to eat hot puddings, which was great profit to the goodwife. Now, to prevent her of this commodity, the vicar spake against it and forbade it openly, yet it was not so deeply inveighed against, but that diverse Sundays they would make a steal thither to breakfast, and one Sunday amongst the rest, the whole crew being gathered together, notice was given to the vicar, whereupon he hied him thither, and found them all hard at it by the teeth.

When they saw mass vicar come in, every man rose up and ran away to shift for himself. The hostess, she whipped in with the puddings, so that there was none left in the house. But Master Vicar, who spying a dozen of lusty large black puddings hanged in the chimney, whipped them into his wide sleeve, and went his way. He was no sooner gone but the goodwife, coming out, missed her puddings and little suspected the vicar, but thought some of her guests had carried them away, whereupon she told it to her husband, who let the matter pass lightly and wished his wife make her hastily ready that they might go to mass. On goes she with her holiday partlet, and sponging herself up, went with her husband to church, and came just to the service.

Well, Master Vicar, who was in a great chafe, mumbled up his Matins, and, after service was done, very stoutly got him into the pulpit, and began to fall to his collation. His text was upon the Gospel for that day, which he coursed and canvassed over, that he fell at last to talk of the breakfast.

'Oh, neighbours,' quoth he, 'as I came this day to churchward, I came into a house, nay, into an alehouse, where I found a crew at breakfast before mass, at a bloody breakfast, a black breakfast. Yea, neighbours, the Devil's breakfast!' And with that, he threw his arms about him with such violence that his wide sleeve untied, the puddings fell out and hit an old wife on the head that she fell over again. The hostess, seeing a dozen of puddings that she missed, cried out to her husband.

'Oh, man,' quoth she, 'there's the dozen of puddings that were gone out of the chimney. Hie thee, lest they be gone!'

At this there was such a laughing and such a rumour that the poor vicar to leave of his collation and come down to answer what the alewife objected against him. But he was so well beloved in the parish, that the alewife was punished, and her Sunday breakfasts put down by a common consent of the churchwardens.

71.　Of the franklin's son that came to take Orders.

A CERTAIN scholar there was, intending to be made a priest, which had neither great wit nor learning, came to the bishop to take Orders. Whose foolishness the bishop perceiving, because he was a rich man's son would
5   not very strongly oppose him, but asked him this small question:

    'Noah had three sons: Shem, Ham and Japheth. Now tell me,' quod the bishop, 'who was Japheth's father, and thou shalt have Orders.'

10   Then said the scholar, 'By my troth, my lord, I pray you pardon me. For I never learned but little of the Bible.'

    Then quod the bishop, 'Go home, and come again and solve me this question, and thou shalt have Orders.'

    This scholar so departed and came home to his father,
15   and showed him the cause of the hindrance of his Orders.

    His father, being angry at his foolishness, thought to teach him the solution of this question by a familiar example, and called his spaniels before him, and said thus:

'Thou knowest well, Coll my dog hath these three   20
whelps, Rig, Trig and Tribble. Must not Coll my dog needs
be sire to Tribble?'

Then quod the scholar, 'By God, father, ye say truth!
Let me alone now. Ye shall see me do well enough the next
time.'   25

Wherefore on the morrow, he went to the bishop again
and said he could solve his question.

Then said the bishop, 'Noah had three sons: Shem, Ham
and Japheth. Now tell me, who was Japheth's father?'

'Marry, sir,' quod the scholar, 'if it please your lordship,   30
Coll, my father's dog.'

*By this tale a man may learn that it is but lost time to teach
a fool anything which hath no wit to perceive it.*

A.69: *Of the frankelyns sonne that cam to take orders.*

B.71: *Of the frankelyns son that cam to take orders.*

franklin: a free landowner—one step down from a gentleman.

to take Orders: to become ordained, to take holy orders (3, *et al.*).

marry: indeed, certainly (30).

The moral is among several which contrast wisdom, learning and orderly behaviour with foolishness, wilfulness and stupidity, *cf.* Tales 1, 5, 8, 34, 37, 67, 69, 73, 75 and 81.

A similar story is told in the *Jests of Scoggin* (1565-6):

After this, the said scholar did come to the next Orders, and brought a present to the ordinary from Scoggin, but the scholar's father paid for all. Then said the ordinary to the scholar, 'I must needs oppose you and, for Master Scoggin's sake, I will oppose you in a light matter. Isaac had two sons, Esau and Jacob. Who was Jacob's father?'

The scholar stood still and could not tell.

'Well,' said the ordinary, 'I cannot admit you to be priest, until the next Orders, and then bring me an answer.'

The scholar went home with a heavy heart, bearing a letter to Master Scoggin, how his scholar could not answer to this question, 'Isaac had two sons, Esau and Jacob. Who was Jacob's father?'

Scoggin said to his scholar, 'Thou fool and ass-head, dost thou not know Tom Miller of Osney?'

'Yes,' said the scholar.

'Then,' said Scoggin, 'thou knowest he had two sons, Tom and Jack. Who is Jack's father?'

The scholar said, 'Tom Miller.'

'Why,' said Scoggin, 'thou mightest have said that Isaac was Jacob's father, then,' said Scoggin. 'Thou shalt arise betime in the morning, and carry a letter to the ordinary, and I trust he will admit thee before the Orders shall be given.'

The scholar rose up betime in the morning, and carried the letter to the ordinary. The ordinary said, 'For Master Scoggin's sake, I will oppose you no further than I did yesterday. Isaac had two sons, Esau and Jacob. Who was Jacob's father?'

'Marry,' said the scholar, 'I can tell you now, that was Tom Miller of Osney.'

'Go, fool, go,' said the ordinary, 'and let thy master send thee no more to me for Orders, for it is unpossible to make a fool a wise man.'

72. Of the husbandman that lodged the friar in his own bed.

IT fortuned so that a friar late in the evening desired lodging of a poor man of the country, the which, for lack of other lodging, glad to harbour the friar, lodged him in his own bed. And after, he and his wife, the friar being asleep, came and lay in the same bed.

And in the morning after, the poor man rose and went to the market, leaving the friar in the bed with his wife. And as he went, he smiled and laughed to himself, wherefore his neighbours demanded of him why he so smiled.

He answered and said, 'I laugh to think how shamefast the friar shall be when he waketh, whom I left in bed with my wife.'

By this tale a man may learn that he that overshooteth himself doth foolishly, yet he is more fool to show it openly.

A.70: *Of the husbandman that lodgyd the frere in his own bede.*
B.72: *Of the husbandman that lodgyd the frere in hys owne bed.*
D.9: *The husband man that, &c.*

husbandman: a tenant farmer or smallholder.

shamefast: ashamed (11).

overshooteth himself: goes beyond his means or abilities (14-5).

73. Of the priest that would say two Gospels for a groat.

SOMETIME there dwelled a priest in Stratford-upon-Avon of small learning, which undevoutly sang Mass and oftentimes twice on one day. So it happened on a time, after his second Mass was done, in Shottery not a
5 mile from Stratford, there met with him diverse merchant men which would have heard Mass, and desired him to sing Mass and he should have a groat.

Which answered them and said, 'Sirs, I will say Mass no more this day, but I will say you two Gospels for one groat,
10 and that is dog cheap a Mass in any place in England!'

By this tale a man may see that they that be rude and unlearned regard but little the merit and goodness of holy prayer.

Stratford-upon-Avon: Stratford-upon-Avon, Warwickshire (1-2, 5).

twice on one day: Canon Law forbids a priest from celebrating Mass more than once a day, except in special circumstances (3).

Shottery: Shottery, Warwickshire (4).

groat: a silver coin worth four pence (4*d.*) the equivalent of about £8.50 today (7, 9).

dog cheap: very cheap, 'dirt cheap' (10).

rude: uneducated, uncouth (11).

The moral is among several which contrast wisdom, learning and orderly behaviour with foolishness, wilfulness and stupidity, *cf.* Tales 1, 5, 8, 34, 37, 67, 69, 71, 75 and 81.

74. Of the courtier that did cast the friar over the boat.

A COURTIER and a friar happened to meet together in a ferry boat and, in communication between them, fell at words angry and displeased each with other, and fought and struggled together so that, at the last, the courtier cast the friar over the boat, and so was the friar drowned.

The ferryman, which had been a man of war the most part of his life before, and seeing the friar was so drowned and gone, said thus to the courtier:

'I beshrew thy heart! Thou shouldst have tarried and fought with him a-land, for now thou hast caused me to lose an halfpenny for my fare.'

By this tale a man may see that he that is accustomed in vicious and cruel company, shall lose that noble virtue to have pity and compassion upon his neighbour.

A.72: *Of the coutear that dyd cast the frere ouer the bote.*
B.74: *Of the courtear that dyd cast the frere ouer the bote.*
D.38: *Of Courtier yat did, &c.*

man of war: a soldier, a mercenary (7).

beshrew: to curse (10).

a-land: on land (11).

halfpenny: a silver coin worth half a penny (½d.) the equivalent of about £1 today (12).

By this tale ...: nowadays, this ex-soldier might be diagnosed with Post-Traumatic Stress Disorder (13-5).

75.   Of the friar that preached
what men's souls were.

A PREACHER in the pulpit which preached the Word of God and, among other matters, spoke of men's souls, and said they were so marvellous and so subtle that a thousand souls might dance in the space of a nail of a
5 man's finger. Among which audience, there was a merry conceited fellow of small devotion, that answered and said thus:

'Master Doctor, if that a thousand souls may dance on a man's nail, I pray you then, where shall the piper stand?'

10 *By this tale a man may see that it is but folly to show or to teach virtue to them that have no pleasure nor mind thereto.*

Master Doctor: the preacher is clearly a university man (8).

piper: probably a bagpiper, but possibly a musician playing three-hole pipe and drum (9).

The moral is among several which contrast wisdom, learning and orderly behaviour with foolishness, wilfulness and stupidity, *cf.* Tales 1, 5, 8, 34, 37, 67, 69, 71, 73 and 81.

This tale is an early parody of the scholasticism practiced in medieval universities, which could include discussion of questions such as 'Can several angels be in the same place?' (Thomas Aquinas, *Summa Theologica*). While he may appreciate the humour of the 'merry conceited fellow,' Rastell also sees merit in the scholastic approach.

In Rastell's interlude, *The Four Elements* (c.1519), the character of Ignorance remarks:
That is the best dance without a pipe
That I saw this seven year.

(lines 1347-8)

76.   Of the husband that cried 'Bleh!' under the bed.

IN London there was a certain artificer having a fair wife, to whom a lusty gallant made pursuit to accomplish his pleasure. This woman, denying, showed the matter unto her husband which, moved therewith, bade his wife to appoint him a time to come secretly to lie with her all night, and with great cracks and oaths swore that, against his coming he would be ready harnessed and would put him in jeopardy of his life, except he would make him a great amends.

This night was then appointed, at which time this courtier came at his hour and entered into the chamber, set his two-hand sword down and said these words:

'Stand thou there, thou sword, the death of three men.'

This husband, lying under the bed in harness, hearing these words lay still for fear. The courtier anon got him to bed with the wife about his prepensed business, and within an hour or two, the husband being weary of lying began to remove him. The courtier that hearing, asked the wife what thing that was that removed under the bed. Which, excusing the matter, said it was a little sheep that was wont daily to go about the house. And the husband that hearing, anon cried 'Bleh!' as it had been a sheep.

And so in conclusion, when the courtier saw his time, he rose and kissed the wife and took his leave and departed. And as soon as he was gone, the husband arose and, when the wife looked on him somewhat abashed, she began to make a sad countenance and said, 'Alas, sir, why did ye not rise and play the man, as ye said ye would?'

Which answered and said, 'Why, dame, didst thou not hear him say that his sword had been the death of three men, and I had been a fool then if that I had put myself in jeopardy to have been the fourth.'

Then said the wife thus: 'But, sir, spoke not I wisely then when I said ye were a sheep?'

'Yes,' quod the husband, 'but then, did not I more wisely, dame, when that I cried, "Bleh!"'

By this ye may see that he is not wise that will put his confidence too much upon these great crackers which oft times will do but little when it cometh to the point.

cracks: boasts, foolish exclamations (6).

against: in expectation of, in readiness for (6).

harnessed: equipped with arms and armour (7).

except: unless (8).

anon: soon, presently, shortly (15, 22).

prepensed: intended, previously conceived (16).

abashed: disconcerted, embarrassed (26).

cracker: a boaster, a braggart (38).

The moral here is similar to that for Tale 42.

From *Cent Nouvelles Nouvelles* (1461-2) attributed to Antoine de la Salle, where a Scottish archer takes the role of the 'lusty gallant'.

77. Of the shoemaker that asked the collier what tidings in Hell.

THERE was a shoemaker sitting in his shop that saw a collier come by, and thought to deride him because he was so black, and asked him what tidings were in Hell and how the Devil fared.

5   To whom the collier said, 'The Devil fared well, when I saw him last, for he was riding forth and tarried but for a souter to pluck on his boots.'

By this ye may see that he that useth to deride other folks is sometime himself more derided and mocked.

A.75: *Of the shomaker that asked the colyer what tydynges in hell.*
B.77: *Of the shomaker that askyd the colyer what tydyngys in hell.*
D.40: *Of the Schomaker &c.*

collier: because of their blackened appearance, underworld mines, and sulphurous smelling fiery wares, colliers were often associated with the Devil—*cf.* Ulpian Fulwell's *'Like will to Like,' quoth the Devil to the Collier,* 1568 (2, 5).

souter: shoemaker (7).

to pluck on: to pull on (7).

The moral is among those which warn that treating others with scorn and derision can sometimes backfire, *cf.* Tales 2, 14, 53, 60 and 82.

A version of this jest reappears in *The Pleasant Conceits of Old Hobson* (1607):

A poor beggar man, that was foul, black and loathsome to behold, came on a time to Master Hobson as he walked in Moorfields, and asked something of him for an alms. To whom Master Hobson said, 'I pray thee fellow, get from me, for thou lookest as thou camest lately out of Hell.'

The poor beggar, perceiving he would give him nothing, answered, 'Forsooth, sir, you say true, for I came lately out of Hell indeed.'

'Why didst not thou tarry there still?' quoth Master Hobson.

'Nay, sir,' quoth the beggar, 'there is no room for such beggarmen as I am, for all is kept for such gentlemen citizen as you be.'

This witty answer caused Master Hobson to give the poor man a tester [a coin valued at sixpence].

78.   Of St Peter that cried, 'Caws pob!'

I FIND written among old gests, how God made St Peter Porter of Heaven, and that God of His Goodness soon after His Passion suffered many men to come to the Kingdom of Heaven with small deserving, at which time there was in Heaven a great company of Welshmen which, with their cracking and babbling, troubled all the other.

Wherefore God said to St Peter that he was weary of them, and that he would fain have them out of Heaven. To whom St Peter said, 'Good Lord, I warrant you that shall be shortly done.'

Wherefore St Peter went out of Heaven Gates and cried with a loud voice, 'Caws pob!' that is as much to say as 'roasted cheese.' Which thing the Welshmen hearing, ran out of Heaven a great pace.

And when St Peter saw them all out, he suddenly went into Heaven and locked the door, and so sparred all the Welshmen out.

By this ye may see that it is no wisdom for a man to love or to set his mind too much upon any delicate or worldly pleasure, whereby he shall lose the celestial and eternal Joy.

A.76: *Of Seynt Peter that cryed cause bobe.*
B.78: *Of seynt Peter that cryed cause bobe.*

Caws pob: baked or roast cheese (Welsh)—*cf.* Andrew Boorde's *Fyrst Boke of the Introduction of Knowledge* (1542), 'I am a Welshman; I do love cause boby, good roasted cheese' (12).

gests: this word, which is essentially the same as 'jests,' is used here with its older meaning of a tale of notable deeds, from Latin *gesta*, 'deeds' (1).

cracking: boasting, noisy or foolish chatter (6).

fain: gladly, wishfully, heartily (8).

shortly: swiftly, speedily (10).

a great pace: very quickly (14).

suddenly: immediately, abruptly (15).

sparred: locked, shut, barred (16).

The moral is one of several concerned with covetousness, miserliness, and attitudes to money and personal possessions, *cf.* Tales 15, 17, 20, 33, 62, 68, 90, 91 and 100.

79. Of him that adventured body and soul for his prince.

TWO knights there were which went to a standing field with their prince. But one of them was confessed before he went, but the other went into the field without shrift or repentance.

5   Afterward, this prince won the field and had the victory that day, wherefore he that was confessed came to the prince and asked an office, and said that he had deserved it, for he had done good service and adventured that day as far as any man in the field.

10   To whom the other that was unconfessed answered and said, 'Nay, by the Mass, I am more worthy to have a reward than he, for he adventured but his body for your sake, for he durst not go to the field till he was confessed but, as for me, I did imperil both body, life and soul for your sake, for 15 I went to the field without confession or repentance.'

A.77: *Of hym that aduenturyd body and soule for hys prynce.*
B.79: *Of hym that aduenturyd body & sowle for hys prynce.*

standing field: a field of battle (1).

shrift: confession (4).

adventured: ventured, risked (8,12).

office: an official position (7).

durst: dared (13).

80.   Of the parson that
stole the miller's eels.

A CERTAIN miller there was which had diverse ponds of eels, wherein was good store of eels. Wherefore the parson of the town, which looked like an holy man, diverse and many times stole many of them, insomuch that he had left few or none behind him. Wherefore this miller, seeing his eels stolen and wist not by whom, came to the said parson and desired him to curse for them.

The parson said he would and, the next Sunday, came into the pulpit with book, bell and candle, and perceiving there were none in the church that understood Latin, said thus:

'He that stole the miller's eels, *laudate Dominum de Caelis*, but he that stole the other eels, *gaudeat ipse in Caelis*,' and therewith put out the candle.

'Why, sir,' quod the miller, 'no more, for this sauce is sharp enough for him!'

By this ye may see that some curates that look full holy be but dissemblers and hypocrites.

A.78: *Of the parson that stale the mylners elys.*
B.80: *Of the parson that stall the mylners elys.*

wist: knew (6).

laudate Dominum de Caelis: 'praise the Lord of Heaven' (12-3).

other: the original text (in 'B') reads 'grer' which Zall takes as a contraction of 'greater', but which may simply be a misreading of manuscript 'oþer' or 'oyer' (13).

gaudeat ipse in Caelis: 'may he himself rejoice in Heaven' (13-4).

curate: a priest charged with the cure or care of souls, a parish priest (17).

The tale is retold in Book XII of Reginald Scot's *The Discovery of Witchcraft* (1584):
   So it was, that a certain Sir John [*i.e.* a priest, *cf.* Tale 2], with some of his company, once went abroad a-jetting, and in a moon-light evening robbed a miller's weir, and stole all his eels. The poor miller made his moan to Sir John himself, who willed him to be quiet, for he would so curse the thief and all his confederates, with bell, book and candle, that they should have small joy of their fish. And therefore the next Sunday, Sir John got him to the pulpit, with his surplice on his back and his stole about his neck, and pronounced these words following in the audience of the people:
   All you that have stolen the miller's eels
   Laudate Dominum de caelis,
   And all they that have consented thereto,
   Benedicamus Domino.
   'Lo,' saith he, 'there is sauce for your eels, my masters!'
Samuel Harsnett alludes to the story in his *A Declaration of Egregious Popish Impostures* (1603), where the 'curse' is attributed to Sir John Grantham.

81. Of the Welshman that saw one forty shillings better than God.

A WELSHMAN on a time went to church to hear Mass, which happened to come in even at the sacring time. When he had heard that Mass to the end, he went home where one of his fellows asked him whether he had seen God Almighty today.

Which answered and said, 'Nay, but I saw one forty shillings better than he!'

By this ye may see that they be evil brought up, have but little devotion to prayer and virtue.

A.79: *Of the Welchman that saw one xl's better than God.*
B.81: *Of the welchman that saw one .xl. shyl. better than god.*

forty shillings: the equivalent of about £1,000 today (6-7).

sacring time: the moment of consecration (2).

fellows: companions, associates, friends (4).

The moral is among several which contrast wisdom, learning and orderly behaviour with foolishness, wilfulness and stupidity, *cf.* Tales 1, 5, 8, 34, 37, 67, 69, 71, 73 and 75.

82.   Of the friar that said 'Dirige' for the hog's soul.

UPON a time, certain women in the country were appointed to deride and mock a friar, a limiter that used much to visit them. Whereupon one of them, a little before that the friar came, killed an hog and for disport laid it under the board after the manner of a corpse, and told the friar it was her good man and desired him to say 'Dirige' for his soul. Wherefore the friar and his fellow began 'Placebo' and 'Dirige', and so forthsaid the Service full devoutly. Which the wives so hearing, could not refrain themself from laughing, and went into a little parlour to laugh more at their pleasure.

These friars somewhat suspected the cause, and quickly, ere that the women were ware, looked under the board and spied that it was an hog, suddenly took it between them and bore it homeward as fast as they might.

The women seeing that, ran after the friar and cried, 'Come again, Master Friar! Come again, and let it alone!'

'Nay, by my Faith,' quod the friar. 'He is a Brother of ours, and therefore he must needs be buried in our cloister.'

And so the friars got the hog.

By this ye may see that they that use to deride and mock other, sometime it turneth to their own loss and damage.

A.80: *Of the frere that said dyryge for the hoggys soule.*
B.82: *Of the frere that sayd dyrige for the hoggys sowle.*
D.41: *The freir yat said dirge for ye.*

'Dirige': Matins for the Dead; see *'Placebo' and 'Dirige'* below (7, 8).

appointed: resolved, decided, agreed (2).

limiter: a friar who paid his convent a fee for the exclusive right to beg within the limits of a fixed district (2).

hog: a swine or pig, specifically a castrated male pig kept for pork or bacon (4, *et al.*).

disport: amusement, fun (4).

board: a table (5, 13).

good man: husband (6).

fellow: a companion (7).

'Placebo' and 'Dirige': Vespers and Matins for the Dead; Vespers for the Dead begins with the antiphon *Placebo Domino*, and Matins with the antiphon *Dirige, Domine* (8).

forthsaid: recited (8).

ere: before (13).

ware: aware (13).

suddenly: immediately, abruptly (14).

come again: come back (17).

The moral is among those which warn that treating others with scorn and derision can sometimes backfire, *cf.* Tales 2, 14, 53, 60 and 77.

83. Of the parson that said Mass of Requiem for Christ's soul.

A CERTAIN priest there was that dwelled in the country, which was not very well learned. Therefore on Easter Eve, he sent his boy to the priest of the next town that was two mile from thence, to know what Mass he should sing on the morrow. This boy came to the said priest, and did his masters errand to him.

Then quod the priest, 'Tell thy master that he must sing tomorrow of the Resurrection,' and furthermore quod he, 'If thou hap to forget it, tell thy master that it beginneth with a great R,' and showed him the Mass Book where it was written, *Resurrexi. etc.*

This boy then went home again and all the way as he went he clattered still, '*Resurrexi, resurrexi,*' but at the last he happened to forget it clean. And when he came home, his master asked him what Mass he should sing on the morrow.

'By my troth, Master,' quod the boy, 'I have forgotten it. But he bade me tell you it began with a great R.'

'By God,' quod the priest, 'I trow thou sayest truth, for now I remember well it must be *Requiem eternam,* for God Almighty died upon Good Friday, and now we must say Mass for his soul.'

By this ye may see that when one fool sendeth another fool on his errand, oftentimes the business is foolishly sped.

A.81: *Of the parson that sayde masse of requiem for Crystes soule.*
B.83: *Of the parson that sayd masse of requiem for Crystys sowle.*

resurrexi: 'I am risen'—the first word of the introit for Easter Day (11, 13).

requiem eternam: 'eternal rest'—the opening words of the Mass for the Dead (20).

sped: fixed up, sorted, carried out (24).

From Heinrich Bebel's *Facetiae* (1506). The tale is retold in the *Jests of Scoggin* (1565-6):
On an Easter day, this aforesaid parson could not tell what Mass he should say, wherefore he said to the clerk, 'I pray thee, run to my next neighbour, the Parson of Garsington, and let him send me word what Mass I shall say today.'

The parson said to the clerk, 'Let him say the Mass which doth begin with a great R.'

The priest turned over his book and found *Requiem eternam*, and said the Mass which is used for a soul or souls. When Mass was done, one said to him, 'Master Parson, for whose soul did you say Mass today?'

'Sir,' said he, 'for God's soul which died on Friday last, for I was sick yesterday and could not say Mass for his soul.'

'Sir,' said the man, 'God is alive and not dead.'

'No?' said he, 'If He had not been dead, He should not have been buried.'

'All this is true,' said the man, 'but after He was dead, He rose from death to life and is alive and shall die no more.'

'By my faith,' said the parson, 'I will never after this pray for Him any more.'

'No,' said the man, 'you must never pray for God, but you must pray to God to send you some wit, or else you will die a fool.'

84.   Of the herdman that said, 'Ride apace, ye shall have rain!'

Ascholar of Oxenford which had studied the judicials of astronomy on a time was riding by the way, which came by a herdman and enquired of him how far it was to the next town.

5 'Sir,' quod the herdman, 'ye have not thither past a mile and a half. But, sir,' quod he, 'ye need to ride apace, for ye shall have a shower of rain ere ye come thither.'

'What!' quod the scholar. 'That is not so, for here is no token of rain, for all the clouds be both fair and clear.'

10 'By God, sir,' quod the herdman, 'but ye shall find it so.'

The scholar then rode forth his way, and ere he had ridden half a mile further, there fell a good shower of rain, that the scholar was well washed and wet to the skin. The scholar then turned his horse and rode again to the

15 herdman and desired him to teach him that cunning.

'Nay,' quod the herdman, 'I will not teach you my cunning for nought.'

Then the scholar proffered him forty shillings to teach him that cunning. The herdman, after he had received his

20 money, said thus: 'Sir, see you not yonder dun-a-cow with the white face?'

'Yes,' quod the scholar.

'Surely,' quod the herdman, 'when she danceth and holdeth up her tail, ye shall have a shower of rain within half an hour after.'   25

By this ye may see that the cunning of herdmen and shepherds as touching alterations of weathers is more sure than the judicials of astronomy.

A.82: *Of the herdeman that sayde: ryde apace, ye shall haue rayn.*
B.84: *Of the herdman that sayd ryde apace ye shall haue rayn.*
D.42: *The Herdman that said, &c.*

Oxenford: Oxford (1).

judicials of astronomy: astrology, here especially denoting the supposed influence of planets on the weather, sometimes regarded as a branch of 'natural astrology' (2, 28).

apace: quickly (6).

ere: before (7, 11).

token: sign (9).

cunning: knowledge (15, *et al.*).

forty shillings: the equivalent of about £1,000 today (18).

dun-a-cow: a dun-coloured cow (20).

surely: certainly, assuredly (23).

This tale is retold in the *Jests of Scoggin* (1565-6):

On a time as Scoggin was riding to the Abbot of Bury, he asked of a cowherd how far it was to Bury. The cowherd said, 'Twenty miles.'

'May I,' said Scoggin, 'ride thither tonight?'

'Yea,' said the cowherd. 'If you ride not too fast and also if you ride not a good pace, you will be wet ere you come half way there.'

As Scoggin was riding on his way, he did see a cloud arise that was black, and being afraid to be wet, he spurred his horse and did ride a great pace, and riding so fast, his horse stumbled and strained his leg, and might not go. Scoggin, revolving in his mind the cowherds words, did set up his horse at a poor man's house, and returned to the cowherd, supposing that he had been a good astronomer because he said, 'if you ride not too fast, you may be at Bury to night,' and also, 'if you do not ride fast, you shall be wet ere you come there.'

Scoggin said to the cowherd, 'What shall I give thee to tell me, when I shall have rain or fair weather?'

'There goeth a bargain!' said the cowherd. 'What wilt thou give me?'

Scoggin said, 'Twenty shillings.'

'Nay,' said the cowherd. 'For forty shillings I will tell you and teach you, but I will be paid first.'

'Hold the money,' said Scoggin.

The cowherd said, 'Sir, do you see yonder cow with the cut tail?'

'Yea,' said Scoggin.

'Sir,' said the cowherd, 'when that she doth begin to set up her rump and draw to a hedge or bush, within an hour after, you shall have rain. Therefore, take the cow with you, and keep her as I do, and you shall ever be sure to know when you shall have fair weather or foul.'

'Nay,' said Scoggin, 'keep thy cow still, and give me twenty shillings of my money.'

'That is of my gentleness,' said the cowherd. 'Howbeit, you seem to be an honest man—there is twenty shillings.'

Here, a man may see that wit is never good till it be bought.

85.   Of him that said,
'I shall have ne'er a penny.'

IN a certain town there was a rich man that lay on his deathbed at point of death, which charged his executors to deal for his soul a certain some of money in pence, and on this condition charged them, as they would answer afore God, that every poor man that came to them and told a true tale should have a penny, and they that said a false thing should have none.

And in the dole time, there came one which said that God was a good man.

Quod the executors, 'Thou shalt have a penny, for thou sayest truth.'

Anon, came another and said the Devil was a good man.

Quod the executors, 'There thou liest, therefore thou shalt have ne'er a penny.'

At last, came one to the executors and said thus:

'Ye shall give me ne'er a penny.'

Which words made the executors amazed, and took advisement whether they should give him the penny or no.

By this ye may see it is wisdom for judges in dutiful matters of law to beware of hasty judgement.

A.83: *Of hym that sayde: I shall haue neuer a peny.*
B.85: *Of him that sayd I shall haue nere a peny.*

ne'er: never (14, 16).

deal: to distribute as alms (3).

in pence: in single pennies—a penny is the equivalent of about £2 today (3).

the dole time: the period when alms are distributed according to the dead man's will (8).

anon: soon, presently, shortly (12).

amazed: bewildered, perplexed (17).

advisement: advice (18).

The moral here may be compared with those of Tales 51, 52 and 94.

86.   Of the husband that said
his wife and he agreed well.

A MAN asked his neighbour, which was but late
married to a widow, how he agreed with his wife,
for he said that her first husband and she could never
agree, by God.

5   Quod the other, 'We agree marvellous well.'

'I pray thee, how so?'

'Marry,' quod the other, 'I shall tell thee. When I am
merry, she is merry, and when I am sad, she is sad. For
when I go out of my doors, I am merry to go from her
10   and so is she. And when I come in again, I am sad and
so is she.'

A.84: *Of the husbande that sayde his wyfe and he agreed well.*

B.86: *Of the husband that sayd his wyfe and he agreed well.*

C.1: [first part missing] *am mery, she is mere & when I am sade,*

D.43: *The husband yat said, &c.*

agree: to be in concord or harmony, to get along together (2, *et al.*).

marry: indeed, certainly (7).

87. Of the priest that said, 'Comede episcope.'

ON the time of Visitation, a bishop, which was somewhat lecherous and had got many children, prepared to come to a priest's house to see what rule he kept. Which priest had a leman in his house called Ede, and by her had two or three small children in short space.

But against the bishop coming, the priest prepared a room to hide his leman and his children over in the roof of his hall. And when the bishop was come and set at dinner in the same hall, having ten of his own children about him, this priest which could speak little Latin or none, bade the bishop in Latin to eat saying, '*Comede, episcope.*'

This woman in the roof of the house hearing the priest say so, had weened he had called her, bidding her 'Come Ede!' and answered shortly and said, 'Shall I bring my children with me also?'

This bishop hearing this, said in sport, '*Uxor tua sicut vitis abundans in lateribus domus tuae.*'

The priest then half amazed answered shortly and said, '*Filii tui sicut novellae olivarum in circuitu mensae tuae.*'

By this ye may see that they that have but small learning sometime speak truly unadvised.

A.85: *Of the prest that sayde Comede episcope.*
B.87: *Of the preest that sayd comede episcope.*
C.2: [no title] *ON the tyme of visitacion a bisshop*

Comede, episcope: 'Eat, bishop!' (11-2).

Visitation: inspection by an ecclesiastical superior (1).

leman: mistress (4,7).

weened: supposed, imagined (14).

Uxor tua sicut vitis abundans in lateribus domus tuae: 'Your wife is like a fruitful vine on the sides of your house' —from Psalm 127:3 (17-8).

shortly: hastily (19).

Filii tui sicut novellae olivarum in circuitu mensae tuae: 'Your children are like young olive trees around your table' —the following words from the same psalm (20).

speak truly unadvised: to speak truth without knowledge; for a similar moral *cf.* Tale 59 (22).

from *Margarita Facetiarum* by Johannes Adelphus, 1508.
The tale is retold in the *Jests of Scoggin* (1565-6):
　　The ordinary said, 'Master Parson, you be complained on because you do keep a young wench in your house.'
　　'Master,' said the parson, 'she is not young, for she is of the age of my horse.'
　　'Why,' said the ordinary, 'how old is your horse?'
　　'Master,' said the parson, 'eighteen years old.'
　　'Well,' said the ordinary, 'you must put away your wench.'
　　'Now,' said the priest, 'I had rather loose my benefice, for then must I brew and bake, and do all things myself, and that I will not do.'
　　'Well,' said the ordinary, 'I will come home to your house one day, and see what rule you keep.'
　　'Sir,' said the parson, 'you shall be welcome.'
　　The ordinary came to the parson's house, and when he did see the wench he said, *'Uxor tua sicut vitis abundans in lateribus domus tuae.'*
　　The parson thought the ordinary had opposed him in our Latin Matins and said, *'Et filii tui sicut novellae olivarum in circuitu mensae tuae.'*
　　The ordinary was abashed, and supposed that some man had told him of his children that he had in his house of his own, sitting round about at his Table, was ashamed to rebuke the parson and said nothing else but, 'Farewell, Master Parson.'
　　Thus a man may perceive that diverse times fools be fortunate, and it is evil and a foolish thing for a man to reprehend another man for a fault that he himself is guilty in.

88. Of the woman that stole the pot.

ON Ash Wednesday in the morning was a curate of a church, which had made good cheer the night afore and sitten up late, and came to the church to hear confession. To whom there came a woman, and among other things, she confessed her that she had stolen a pot. But then, because of great watch that this priest had, he there suddenly fell asleep, and when this woman saw him not willing to hear her, she rose up and went her way.

And anon, another woman kneeled down to the same priest, and began to say 'Benedicite.' Wherewith this priest suddenly awaked, weening she had been the other woman, and said all angrily, 'What, art thou now at "Benedicite" again? Tell me, what didst thou, when thou hadst stolen the pot?'

A.86: *Of the woman that stale the pot.*
B.88: *Of the woman that stale the pot.*
C.3: [no title] *ON assh wednysday in the morning*

Ash Wednesday: the first of 40 days of abstinence during Lent; the preceding day, Shrove Tuesday, was celebrated as a last opportunity for indulgence (1).

curate: a priest charged with the cure or care of souls, a parish priest (1).

watch: a lack of sleep (6).

suddenly: instantly, immediately, abruptly (7, 11).

anon: soon, presently, shortly (9).

Benedicite: 'Bless me' —spoken by the penitent as the preliminary to Confession (10, 13).

weening: supposing, imagining, assuming (11).

285

89.   Of Master Whittington's dream.

SOON after one Master Whittington had builded a
college, on a night as he slept, he dreamed that he sat
in his church and many folks there also. And further he
dreamed that he saw Our Lady in the same church, with a
glass of goodly ointment in her hand, going to one asking
him what he had done for her sake, which said that he had
said Our Lady's Psalter every day, wherefore she gave him
a little of the oil. And anon, she went to another asking
him what he had done for her sake, which said that he had
said two Lady's Psalters every day, wherefore Our Lady
gave him more of the ointment than she gave the other.

This Master Whittington then thought that when Our
Lady should come to him, she would give him all the
whole glass because that he had builded such a great
college, and was very glad in his mind.

But when Our Lady came to him, she asked him what
he had suffered for her sake, which words made him
greatly abashed because he had nothing to say for himself.
And so he dreamed that, for all the great deed of building
of the said college, he had no part of that goodly ointment.

*By this ye may see that to suffer for God's sake is more
meritorious than to give great goods.*

Master Whittington: Sir Richard Whittington (c.1354-1423) is best known today through the tale of Dick Whittington; as Mayor of London, he was able to restore the City's traditional liberties in 1397 (1, 12).

college: in his will, Whittington made provision for the foundation of The College of St Spirit and St Mary, a college of secular priests attached to the church of St Michael Paternoster, with associated almshouses; his bequest, administered by the Mercers' Company, still provides homes for those in need to this day (2, *et al.*).

his church: Whittington paid for the rebuilding and extension of St Michael Paternoster in 1409; Whittington's church was destroyed in the Great Fire of 1666 (3).

Our Lady's Psalter: the prayers of the Rosary (7, 10).

anon: soon, presently, shortly (8).

abashed: disturbed, disconcerted (18).

90. Of the priest that killed his horse called Modicum.

A CERTAIN bishop appointed to go on Visitation to a priest's house and, because he would have the priest do but little cost upon him, he bade him dress but little meat, saying thus in Latin: *Prepare mihi modicum.*

5   This priest, which understood him not half well, had a horse called Modicum. Wherefore he thought to obtain the bishop's favour and, against the bishop's coming, killed his horse that was called Modicum, whereof the bishop and his servants ate part. Which, when the bishop
10   knew afterward, was greatly displeased.

By this ye may see that many a fool doth much cost in making great dinners, which hath but little thank for his labour.

A.88: *Of the prest that killed his horse called modicus.*
B.90: *Of the prest that kyllyd hys horse callyd modicum.*
C.4: [first part missing] *hys seruauntes eate parte, which when*
D.44: *The priest yat killed his hors.*

appointed: resolved, decided, agreed (1).

Visitation: inspection by an ecclesiastical superior (1).

do but little cost: to not spend much money (3).

Prepare mihi modicum: 'Prepare me little,' *i.e.* 'Don't make too much for me' (4).

greatly displeased: horse meat was considered unfit for Christians to eat, having been banned in the eighth century by Pope Gregory III (10).

The moral is one of several concerned with covetousness, miserliness, and attitudes to money and personal possessions, *cf.* Tales 15, 17, 20, 33, 62, 68, 78, 91 and 100.

91.   Of the maltman of Colnbrook.

A CERTAIN maltman of Colnbrook, which was a very covetous wretch and had no pleasure but only to get money, came to London to sell his malt and brought with him four capons, and there received four or five pounds
5   for malt and put it in a little purse tied to his coat, and after went about the streets to sell his capons. Whom a polling fellow that was a dicer and an unthrift had espied, and imagined how he might beguile the man either of his capons or of his money, and came to this maltman in the
10   street bearing these capons in his hand, and asked him how he would sell his capons, and when he had showed him the price of them, he bade him go with him to his master, and he would show them to his master and he would cause him to have money for them, whereto he agreed.

15   This poller went to the Cardinal's Hat in Lombard Street, and when he came to the door he took the capons from the maltman, and bade him tarry at the door till he had showed his master, and he would come again to him and bring him his money for them.

20   This poller, when he had gotten the capons, went into the house and went through the other back entry into Cornhill, and so took the capons with him. And when this maltman had stood there a good season, he asked one of the taverners where the man was that had the capons to
25   show to his master.

'Marry,' quod the taverner, 'I cannot tell thee. Here is neither master nor man in this house, for this entry here is a common highway and goeth into Cornhill. I am sure he is gone away with thy capons.'

This maltman hearing that, ran through the entry into Cornhill and asked for a fellow in a tawny coat that had capons in his hand. But no man could tell him which way he was gone, and so the maltman lost his capons, and after went into his inn all heavy and sad, and took his horse to the intent to ride home.

This poller by that time had changed his raiment and borrowed a furred gown, and came to the maltman sitting on horseback, and said thus: 'Good man, methought I heard thee enquire even now for one in a tawny coat that had stolen from thee four capons. If thou wilt give me a quart of wine, go with me and I shall bring thee to a place where he sitteth drinking with other fellows, and had the capons in his hand.'

This maltman being glad thereof, granted him to give him the wine because he seemed to be an honest man, and went with him unto the Dagger in Cheapside. This poller then said to him, 'Go thy way straight to the end of that long entry, and there thou shalt see whether it be he or no, and I will hold thy horse here till thou come again.'

This maltman, thinking to find the fellow with his capons, went in and left his horse with the other at the door. And as soon as he was gone into the house, this poller led the horse away into his own lodging.

This maltman enquired in the house for his fellow with
the capons, but no man could tell him no tidings of such
man. Wherefore he came again to the door all sad, and
looked for him that had his horse to keep, and because he
saw him not, he asked diverse there for him. And some
said they saw him, and some said they saw him not, but
no man could tell which way he was gone. Wherefore he
went home to his inn, more sad than he was before.
Wherefore his host gave him counsel to get him home,
and beware how he trusted any men in London. This
maltman seeing none other comfort went his high way
homeward.

This poller which lingered alway there about the inn,
heard tell that the maltman was going homeward afoot,
apparelled him like a man's prentice and got a little budget
stuffed full of stones on his back, and went before him to
Charing Cross and tarried till the maltman came, and asked
him whither he went, which said, 'To Colnbrook.'

'Marry,' quod the other, 'I am glad thereof, for I must go
to Brentford to my master, to bear him money which I
have in my budget, and I would be glad of company.'

This maltman, because of his own money, was glad of
his company, and so they agreed and went together a
while. At the last, this poller went somewhat before to
Knightsbridge, and sat upon the bridge and rested him
with his budget on his back. And when he saw the
maltman almost at him, he let his budget fall over the
bridge into the water, and incontinent start up and said

to the maltman, 'Alas, I have let my budget fall into the water, and there is forty pounds of money therein. If thou wilt wade into the water and go seek it and get it me again, I shall give thee twelve pence for thy labour.' 85

This maltman having pity of his loss, and also glad to get the twelve pence, plucked off his hose, coat and shirt, and waded into the water to seek for the budget. And in the meanwhile, this poller got his clothes and coat whereto the purse of money was tied, and leapt over the 90 hedge and went to Westminster.

This maltman, within a while after, with great pain and deep wading, found the budget and came out of the water and saw not his fellow there, and saw that his clothes and money were not there as he left them, suspected the 95 matter and opened the budget and then found nothing therein but stones, cried out like a madman and ran all naked to London again, and said, 'Alas, alas! Help, or I shall be stolen. For my capons be stolen. My horse is stolen. My money and clothes be stolen, and I shall be 100 stolen myself!' And so ran about the streets in London, naked and mad, crying always, 'I shall be stolen! I shall be stolen!' And so continued mad during his life, and so died like a wretch to the utter destruction of himself and shame to all his kin. 105

By this tale ye may see that many a covetous wretch that loved his goods better than God and setteth his mind inordinately thereon, by the right judgement of God oft times cometh to a miserable and shameful end.

maltman: a maker and seller of malt for brewing ale or beer (1, *et al.*).

Colnbrook: now a dependent village of Slough, Berkshire, Colnbrook was then in the county of Buckinghamshire, and was on the main road to Windsor and Bath (1, 71).

capons: neutered cockerels reared for their excellent meat (4, *et al.*).

four or five pounds: the equivalent of about £2,000 to £2,500 today (4).

a polling fellow: a conman, a cheat (7).

dicer: a gambler (7).

unthrift: good-for-nothing (7).

poller: a conman, a cheat (15, *et al.*).

Cardinal's Hat: a pub or tavern that once stood near the meeting of Lombard Street and Cornhill (15).

Lombard Street: this London street takes its name from the Lombard bankers who operated there during the thirteenth and fourteenth centuries (15-6).

marry: indeed, certainly (26, 73).

Cornhill: this street, which runs diagonal to Lombard Street and joins it at Bank Junction, was the site of London's medieval corn market (22, *et al.*).

raiment: clothing, apparel (36).

methought: it seemed to me (38).

tawny: a brownish shade, fashionable in dyed clothes for all ranks (31, 39).

quart: a quarter of a gallon, or two pints—a sixteenth-century pint measured 16 fl oz (473 ml) so a quart was 32 fl oz (946 ml) (41).

The Dagger: a popular pub or tavern on Cheapside at the corner of Foster Lane (46).

Cheapside: the main market street of medieval London (46).

prentice: an indentured servant, an apprentice (68).

budget: a kind of bag commonly used by travellers (68, *et al.*).

Charing Cross: the medieval cross commemorating Queen Eleanor of Castile (d.1290) stood at the western end of The Strand, where it was passed by travellers heading west from London; the cross was demolished in 1647 (70).

Brentford: now part of the London Borough of Hounslow, Brentford was then the county town of Middlesex (73).

because of his own money: the maltman is concerned that he could be robbed if he travels alone (75).

Knightsbridge: then a hamlet outside London, where a bridge crossed the River Westbourne (78).

incontinent: straight away, immediately (81).

forty pounds: the equivalent of about £20,000 today (83).

twelve pence: the equivalent of about £25 today (85, 87).

The moral is one of several concerned with covetousness, miserliness, and attitudes to money and personal possessions, *cf.* Tales 15, 17, 20, 33, 62, 68, 78, 90 and 100.

This story presents particular difficulties for modern readers. While our sense of worldly justice insists that the maltman should be rewarded over the cheat, this story is concerned with heavenly justice; for the purposes of the maltman's story, the cheat is merely an instrument of Divine justice, and so his fate is disregarded. In the end, sin triumphs so completely over the maltman's soul that he runs mad, and his madness allows him little or no hope of future absolution.

There is not much that can be seen as merry about this tale. It was not part of the original collection of tales in 'A' and is unlikely to have reappeared in subsequent editions.

92. Of the Welshman that stole the Englishman's cock.

A WELSHMAN dwelling in England fortuned to steal an Englishman's cock, and set it on the fire to seethe. Wherefore this Englishman, suspecting the Welshman, came into his house and saw the cock seething on the fire, and said to the Welshman thus:

'Sir, this is my cock.'

'Marry,' quod the Welshman, 'and if it be thine, thou shalt have thy part of it.'

'Nay,' quod the Englishman, 'that is not enough.'

'By Cot's Plut and Her Nail,' quod the Welshman, 'if her be not enough now, her will be enough anon, for her hath a good fire under her.'

A.89: *Of the Welcheman that stale the Englysshmans cocke.*
B.92: *Of the welchman that stale the englyshmans cok.*
C.5: [no title] *A Welshman dwellyng in Englande*

seethe: to boil (2).

marry: indeed, certainly (7).

Cot's Plut and Her Nail: God's Blood and His [Crucifixion] Nail—in imitation of the Welshman's accent (10).

enough: the Welshman mistakes the Englishman's meaning, and assumes he means the cock is not well enough cooked—*cf.* Tale 66, line 4 (9,11).

anon: soon, presently, shortly (11).

93. Of him that brought a bottle to a priest.

CERTAIN of the vicars of Paul's, disposed to be merry on a Sunday at High Mass time, sent another mad fellow of their acquaintance unto a foolish, drunken priest to give him a bottle. Which man met with the priest upon the top of the stairs by the chancel door, and spoke to him and said thus:

'Sir, my master hath sent you a bottle to put your drink in, because ye can keep none in your brains.'

This priest therewith being very angry, all suddenly took the bottle and, with his foot, flung it down into the body of the church upon the gentlemen's heads.

A.90: *Of hym that brought a botell to a preste.*
B.93: *Of hym that brought a botell to a prest.*
C.6: [no title] *CErtayne of vicars of Poules dys-*

vicars: priests, agents of a bishop (1).

Paul's: St Paul's Cathedral (1).

suddenly: abruptly, immediately (9).

94. Of the Indictment of Jesu of Nazareth.

A CERTAIN jury in the County of Middlesex was empanelled for the king, to enquire of all indictments, murders and felonies. The persons of this panel were foolish, covetous and unlearned, for whosoever would give them a groat they would assign and verify his bill, whether it were true or false, without any other proof or evidence. Wherefore one that was a merry conceited fellow, perceiving their small conscience and great covetousness, put in a bill entitled after this manner: *Inquiratur pro domino rege si Jesus Nazarenus furatus est unum asinum ad equitandum in Egyptum,* and gave them a groat and desired that it might be verified.

The said jury, which looked all on the groat and nothing on the bill, as was their use, wrote '*billa vera*' on the back thereof. Which bill, when it was presented into the court, when the judges looked thereon, they said openly before all the people, 'Lo, sirs, here is the marvellest verdict that ever was presented by any inquest, for here they have indicted Jesus of Nazareth for stealing of an ass!'

Which when the people heard it, it made them both to laugh and to wonder at the foolishness and shameful perjury of them of the inquest.

By this ye may see it is great peril to empanel any jurors upon any inquest which be foolish and have but small conscience.

A.91: *Of the endytement of Jesu of Nazareth.*
B.94: *Of the endytement of Jhesu of Nazareth.*
C.7: [no title] *A Certayne Jury in the countye of*

groat: a silver coin worth four pence (4*d*.) the equivalent of about £8.50 today (5, *et al.*).

Inquiratur pro domino Rege . . . in Egyptum: 'It is to be enquired for the king, whether Jesus of Nazareth stole a donkey to ride into Egypt' (10-1).

billa vera: 'the bill is true,' endorsing the indictment (14).

marvellest: most marvellous (17).

95.   Of him that preached against them that rode on the Sunday.

IN a certain parish a friar preached, and in his sermon he rebuked them that rode on the Sunday, ever looking upon one man that was booted and spurred, ready to ride. This man, perceiving that all the people noted him, suddenly, half-in-anger answered the friar thus:

'Why preachest thou so much against them that ride on the Sunday, for Christ himself did ride on Palm Sunday, as thou knowest well it is written in Holy Scripture.'

To whom the friar suddenly answered and said thus:

'But I pray thee, what came thereof? Was he not hanged on the Friday after?'

Which hearing, all the people in the church fell on laughing.

A.92: *Of the frere that preched agaynst them that rode on the Sonday.*
B.95: *Of hym that prechyd agaynst theym that rode on the sonday.*
C.8: [no title] *IN a certayne parysshe a frere prea-*

he rebuked them that rode on the Sunday: Sunday is traditionally observed in Christianity as the Sabbath, and is set aside as a day of rest; according to Exodus 20:10, the injunction against working on the Sabbath extends to 'your beast of burden' (*iumentum tuum*), while Deuteronomy 5:14 includes 'your ox, and your ass, and all your beasts of burden' (*bos et asinus et omne iumentum tuum*) (2).

booted and spurred: wearing boots and spurs (3).

suddenly: immediately (5, 9).

96.   Of the one brother that found a purse.

THERE was a certain man that had two sons unlike of conditions. For the eldest was lusty and quick, and used much to rise early and walk into the fields; then was the younger slow and unlusty, and used to lie in his bed as long as he might.

So on a day, the elder, as he was wont, rose early and walked into the fields, and there by fortune he found a purse of money and brought it home to his father. His father, when he had it, went straight to his other son yet lying then in his bed, and said to him, 'O thou sluggard,' quod he, 'seest thou not thine elder brother, how he by his early rising had found a purse with money, whereby we shall be greatly holpen all our life, while thou, slugging in thy bed, dost no good but sleep.'

He then wist not what to say, but answered shortly and said, 'Father,' quod he, 'if he that hath lost the purse and money had lain in his bed that same time that he lost it as I do now, my brother had found no purse nor money today.'

By this ye may see that they that be accustomed in vice and sin will alway find one excuse or other to cloak therewith their vice and unthriftiness.

A.93: Of the one broder that founde a purs.
B.96: Of the one brother that founde a purs.
C.9: [no title] THere was a certaine man that had

conditions: natures, habits, dispositions (2).

lusty: vigorous, energetic (2).

quick: lively (2).

unlusty: slothful, idle, listless (4).

sluggard: an idler, a lay-about (10).

holpen: helped (13).

slugging: lazing about (13).

wist: knew (15).

shortly: promptly, hastily (15).

unthriftiness: dissoluteness, lack of virtue (22).

97. Of the answer of
the mistress to the maid.

A CERTAIN wife there was which was somewhat fair and, as all women be that be fair, was somewhat proud of her beauty and, as she and her maid sat together, she as one that was desirous to be praised, said to her thus:

5 'I'faith, Joan, how thinkest thou? Am I not a fair wife?'

'Yes, by my troth, mistress,' quod she. 'Ye be the fairest that ever was, except Our Lady.'

'Why, by Christ!' quod the mistress. 'Though Our Lady were good, yet she was not so fair as men speak of.'

10 *By this ye may see it is hard to find a beauteous woman without pride.*

maid: an unmarried female servant (3).

i'faith: truly, 'in (good) faith' (5).

fair: beautiful (5, 9).

Our Lady: the Virgin Mary (7, 8).

The moral is one of several concerned with the nature and status of women, *cf.* Tales 3, 10, 11, 19, 23, 29, 35, 46, 49, 58 and 66.

98.   Of a certain alderman's deeds of London.

A CERTAIN alderman of London there was, lately deceased which now shall be nameless, which was very covetous, as well before he was married as after. For when he was bachelor, ever when his hosen were broken so that he could wear them no longer for shame, then would he cut them off by the knee and put on a pair of leather buskins on his bare legs, which would last him a two or three year. Furthermore, it was his manner when he was a bachelor, every night where that he was, to borrow a candle's end to bring him home, which he would alway put in a chest that he had at his chamber. So that by that time he was married, he had a chest of candle's ends that weighed two or three hundredweight.

Soon after that, he was married to a rich widow, and then folks thought he would be better than he was before. But so it happened that a gentleman gave him a pasty of an hart, which every day he caused to be set on the table for service. Howbeit, he would never for niggardship let it be opened, so that it was a month or six weeks ere ever it was touched.

At which time, it fortuned a man of his acquaintance being there often, and seeing this pasty never to be opened, said, 'Sir, by my troth, I will taste your pasty!' Which opened the pasty, and incontinent leapt out three or four mice upon either gentlemen's trenchers, which had crept in at an hole underneath the bottom and had eaten up all the meat therein.

Also this alderman was of such condition that he would hear two or three Masses every day, and when any poor folk came to beg of him, he would rebuke them and say that they did let him in hearing of them, so that he would never give penny in alms.

And on a time as he sat at St Thomas of Acres hearing Mass, he saw a young beginner, a debtor of his that owed him twenty pounds, which as soon as he saw him, he commanded one of his servants to get a sergeant and to arrest him. Which young man immediately after was arrested, and when he was in the counter, he desired diverse of his friends to entreat with this alderman for days of payment. Which men, in the morning after, came to this alderman kneeling at Mass and entreated him for this man, desiring him to take days of payment. Which answered them thus:

'I pray you, trouble me not now, for I have heard one
45 Mass already and I will hear another ere I meddle with
worldly matters. But if ye have the money here, I will take
that now, or else, I pray you, speak to me no more.'

And so these men could get no other answer.

And this alderman kept this young man still in prison
50 till, at the last, he there died. And so he caused likewise
diverse other to die in prison and would never forgive
them, wherefore afterward this alderman died suddenly,
wherefore diverse and many were glad of his death.

alderman of London: a London councillor, responsible for one of the city wards; it has not been possible to identify this alderman with certainty (1, *et al.*).

hosen: stockings, men's hose were commonly joined at the top like trousers (4).

buskins: footed leather stockings or soft boots reaching to below the knee (7).

a pasty of an hart: a venison pasty (16-7).

niggardship: niggardliness, miserliness (*cg.* ON *nigla*, to niggle, to fuss over little things) (18).

ere: before (19, 45).

incontinent: straight away, immediately (24).

trenchers: plates, dishes (25).

let: to hinder, to prevent (31).

hearing of them: i.e. hearing Mass (31).

St Thomas of Acres: the medieval church and hospital of St Thomas of Acre on Cheapside marked the birthplace of St Thomas Beckett, and became closely associated with the Mercers' Company; it was destroyed in the Great Fire of 1666 (33).

beginner: novice, probably a junior lawyer (34).

twenty pounds: the equivalent of about £10,000 today (35).

sergeant: a corps of thirty sergeants-at-arms operated in London (36).

counter: a 'compter' or small prison, in this case either Poultry Counter or Bread Street Counter (38).

days of payment: a period to allow the debtor to raise the necessary money (40, 42).

meddle with: to be concerned with, to engage in (45).

suddenly: unexpectedly (52).

As with Tale 91, there is very little that is merry about this tale. It was not part of the original collection of tales in 'A' and is unlikely to have reappeared in subsequent editions.

99.   Of the northern man
that was all heart.

A NORTHERN man there was which went to seek him
a service. So it happened, that he came to a lord's
place, which lord then had war with another lord. This
lord then asked this northern man if that he durst fight.

5   'Yea, by Good's Banes,' quod the northern man, 'that I
dare, for I is all heart!'

Whereupon, the lord retained him into his service.

So after, it happened that this lord should go fight
with his enemies, with whom also went this northern

10   man, which shortly was smitten in the heel with an
arrow, wherefore he incontinently fell down almost
dead. Wherefore one of his fellows said, 'Art thou he
that art all heart, and for so little a stroke in the heel
now art almost dead?'

15   To whom he answered and said, 'By Good's Sowl, I is all
heart—head, legs, body, heels and all! Therefore ought
not one to fear, when he is stricken in the heart?'

A.95: *Of the northern man that was all harte.*
B.99: *Of the northern man that was all hart.*
C.10: [first part missing] *fell downe almoste deade, Wherfore one.*
D.45: *The Sowthernman that, &c.*

service: a position as servant or retainer (2, 7).

place: manor house, palace (3).

durst: dared (4).

Good's Banes: God's Bones—in imitation a northern accent (5).

shortly: promptly (10).

incontinently: straight away, immediately (11).

Good's Sowl: God's Soul—in imitation a northern accent (15).

100. Of the burning of Old John.

IN a certain town there was a wife somewhat aged, that
had buried her husband whose name was called John,
whom she loved so tenderly in his life, that after his death
she caused an image of timber to be made, in visage and
person as like to him as could be. Which image all day
long lay under her bed, and every night she caused her
maid to wrap it in a sheet and lay it in her bed, and called
it 'Old John.'

This wife also had a prentice whose name was John,
which John would fain have wedded his mistress, not for
no great pleasure but only for her goods because she was
rich. Wherefore he imagined how he might obtain his
purpose, and spoke to the maid of the house and desired
her to lay him in his mistress' bed for one night instead
of the picture, and promised her a good reward for her
labour. Which maid overnight wrapped the said young
man in a sheet and laid him in his mistress' bed as she was
wont to lay the picture.

This widow was wont every night before she slept, and
diverse times when she waked, to kiss the said picture of
Old John, wherefore the said night she kissed the said
young man, believing that she had kissed the picture. And
he suddenly start and took her in his arms, and so well
pleased her then, that Old John from thenceforth was
clean out of her mind, and was content that this young

John should lie with her still all that night, and that the picture of Old John should lie still under the bed for a thing of nought.

After this in the morning, this widow intending to please this young John which had made her so good pastime all the night, bade her maid go dress some good meat for their breakfast to feast therewith her young John. This maid when she had long sought for wood to dress the said meat, told her mistress that she could find no wood that was dry except only the picture of Old John that lieth under the bed.

Then quod the wife again, 'Fetch him down and lay him on the fire, for I see well he will never do me good nor he will never do better service though I keep him never so long.'

So the maid by her commandment dressed the breakfast, and so Old John was cast out for nought and burnt, and from thenceforth young John occupied his place.

By this tale ye may see it is no wisdom for a man to keep long or to cherish that thing that is able to do no pleasure nor service.

maid: an unmarried female servant (7, *et al.*).

prentice: an indentured servant, an apprentice (9).

fain: gladly, wishfully, heartily (10).

picture: a likeness, an artistic representation, not necessarily a drawing or painting (15, *et al.*).

overnight: before nightfall (16).

suddenly: immediately, unexpectedly (23).

start: jumped, leapt up, awoke (23).

dress: to cook (31, *et al.*).

The moral is one of several concerned with covetousness, miserliness, and attitudes to money and personal possessions, *cf.* Tales 15, 17, 20, 33, 62, 68, 78, 90 and 91.

101.   Of the courtier that
ate the hot custard.

A CERTAIN merchant and a courtier were sitting together at a table at dinner, having a hot custard before them. This courtier being somewhat homely of manners took a spoonful of the custard and put it in his
5   mouth, which was so hot that it made his eyes to water.

This merchant, looking on him, thought that he had wept and asked the courtier why he wept.

This courtier, not willing to be known that he had burnt his mouth with the hot custard, answered and said, 'Sir,'
10   quod he, 'I weep because I had a brother which did a certain offence wherefore he was hanged, and because I think now upon his death, it maketh me to weep.'

This merchant thought he had said true and, anon after, the merchant was disposed to eat of the said custard, and
15   took and put a spoonful of it in his mouth, and burnt his mouth also that his eyes watered.

This courtier, that perceiving, spake to the merchant and said, 'Sir,' quod he, 'I pray you, why do ye weep now?'

The merchant perceived how he had beguiled him,
20   answered and said, 'Marry,' quod he, 'I weep, because thou wast not hanged, when thy brother was hanged.'

A.97: *Of the courtear that ete the hot custarde.*
C.11: [no title] *A Certayne marchaunt & a courtyer*
D.46: *The Courteur that did, &c.*

custard: a tart or pie, a custard tart (2, *et al.*).

homely: mild, tame, meek (3).

anon: soon, presently, shortly (13).

marry: indeed, certainly (20).

One of three tales that are omitted from 'B', but which are known from 'A' and from later editions.

102. Of the three points belonging to a shrewd wife.

A YOUNG man that was desirous to have a wife, came to a company of wise philosophers which were gathered together, requiring them to give him some instruction how he might choose him such a wife

5 that were no shrew.

The philosophers, with great study and deliberation, determined and showed this man that there was three special points, whereby he should surely know if a woman were a shrew.

10 The first point is that, if a woman have a shrill voice, it is a great token that she is a shrew.

The second point is that, if a woman have a sharp nose, then most commonly she is a shrew.

The third point is, that never miss, that if she wear

15 kerchiefs, ye may be sure she is a shrew.

A.99: *Of the thre pointes belonging to a shrewd wyfe.*
C.12: [no title] *A Yonge man that was desyrous to*
D.47: *Of thre points belanging, &c.*

shrewd: shrewish, scolding.

shrew: a scolding wife (5, *et al.*).

kerchief: a woman's headcloth, although sometimes costly and elaborate, the same basic garment was worn by all ranks of society—married women were expected to cover their hair, and the kerchief was perhaps recognised as their typical head covering (15).

One of three tales that are omitted from 'B', but which are known from 'A' and from later editions.

103. Of the man that painted the lamb upon his wife's belly.

A CUNNING painter there was dwelling in London, which had a fair young wife, and for things that he had to do, went oversea. But because he was somewhat jealous, he prayed his wife to be content that he might paint a lamb upon her belly, and prayed her that it might remain there till he came home again, wherewith she was content. After which lamb so painted, he departed.

And soon after that, a lusty young merchant, a bachelor, came and wooed his wife, and obtained her favour, so that she was content he should lie with her, which resorted to her and had his pleasure oft times. And on a time he took a pencil, and to the lamb he painted two horns, weening to the wife that he had but refreshed the old painting.

Then at the last, about a year after, her husband came home again, and the first night he lay with his wife, he looked upon his wife's belly, and saw the two horns painted there. He said to his wife, that some other body had been busy there and made a new painting, for the picture that he painted had no horns, and this hath horns.

To whom this wife shortly answered and said, 'Yea, sir, remember that it is a year past and more since ye went, and though it were but a lamb when ye went, now perdie it must needs be a sheep and have horns by the course of nature, and therefore ye must be content.'

This man, hearing his wife's reasonable answer, held him content and asked no more.

cunning: skilful (1).

pencil: a small brush, straw, reed *etc.* used in painting or manuscript illumination (12).

horns: horns are a conventional symbol of cuckoldry (12, *et al.*).

weening to the wife: leading her to believe (12-3).

shortly: promptly, speedily (20).

perdie: by God—French, *'par Dieu'* (22).

One of three tales that are omitted from 'B', but which are known from 'A' and from later editions. This tale is the secular equivalent of Tale 67, 'Of the penitent that said, 'The Sheep of God have mercy upon me.''

FINIS.

Thus endeth the book of
A Hundred Merry Tales.

Johannes · Rastell ⁊

ℂCum pꝛeuilegio
Regali.

Devices from the final page of the second edition ('B') of 1526,
reproduced from the facsimile edition of 1887.

Appendix: Textual variants

The variants listed below include only those differences which have seemed in some way either potentially interesting or significant; general spelling differences and minor typographical errors are not usually included. Abbreviations have been expanded, but it should be remembered that the type representing 'that' (as 'y^t') is easily mistaken for the type for 'the' (as 'y^e') and similarly, some variants may result from the accidental substitution of a type with or without a macron.

Tale 3 (A.2, B.3)

8, 'to you' (B): absent in A.

9, 'hath' (A): B, 'has'.

22, 'didst' (B): A, 'did'.

25, 'into' (A): B, 'to'.

41, 'she' (A): B, 'me'.

Tale 4 (A.3, B.4, D.2)

4, 'mile' (A, B): D, 'myles'.

9, 'the way' (A, B): D, 'that way'.

12, 'other' (A, B): absent in D.

16, 'where' (A, D): B, 'wherin'.

17, 'his' (A, D): B, 'this'.

20, 'ran away' (A, B): D, 'thay ran all away'.

21, 'and because' (A, B): D, 'becaus'.

23, 'that with' (A, B): B, '⁊ wyth'.

24, 'broken' (A, D): B, 'broke'.

29, 'leaped' (A, D): B, 'lepe'.

31, 'thank' (A, B): D, 'thanks'.

32, 'gates' (A, B): D, 'ʒet'.

32, 'To whom' (A, B): D, 'and'.

36, 'sparred' (A, B): D, 'barred'.

36, 'in to' (A, B): D, 'vnto'.

37, 'to' (A, B): D, 'vnto'.

39, 'say' (A, B): D, 'tell'.

41-2, 'This second ... was there.' (A, B): absent in D.

46, 'also' (B): absent in D.

48, 'Master' (B): absent in D.

55, 'chinks' (B): D, 'chaines'.

56, 'the Devil' (B): D, 'a deuil'.

57, 'hanging ... saw' (B): D, 'saw vpon the sadel torris'.

59, 'By God's Body' (B): D, 'sweiring'.

62, 'your soul' (A, B): D, 'it'.

63, 'your soul' (A, B): D, 'it'.

64, 'This' (B): D, 'The'.

64, 'then marvellously abashed' (A, B): D, 'heiring this, was meruelously afraide, and'

64, 'up' (B): absent in A and D.

65, 'to' (B, D): absent in A.

65, 'got' (B, D): A, 'gette'.

66, 'of his' (B): absent in D.

74, 'of me' (B): absent in D.

80, 'by his voice they' (B): 'they' absent in A and D.

83, 'disport' (A, B): D, 'sport'.

Tale 5 (A.4, B.5, D.3)

2, 'like' (B, D): absent in A.

5, 'because' (A, D): B, 'for that that'.

8, 'full well' (A, B): absent in D.

10, 'Soon after' (A, B): D, 'Sone efter that'.

10, 'to him' (A, B): absent in D.

12, 'been' (D): A, B 'be'.

12, 'I give thee' (A, D): B, 'ⅅ I geue the'.

13, 'also I' (B): absent in D.

15, 'ye' (B): A, 'you'; D, 'zow'.

18, 'Anon after' (B): D, 'Anon efter that'.

21, 'wouldst' (D): B, 'wolde'.

24, 'to' (B): D, 'vnto'.

25, 'the' (B): D, 'his'.

28, 'that' (B): absent in D.

28, 'this third son' (B): D, 'this thrid Son so'.

Tale 6 (A.5, B.6)

9, 'challenged it' (B): A, 'and chalenged it'.

13, 'and the other' (A): B, 'the other'.

17, 'the' (A): absent in B.

15, 'met' (B): A, 'dyd mete'.

Tale 8 (A.6, B.8, D.4)

4, 'used that season' (A 'used that …', B):
  D, 'vsed in that sesoun'.

5, 'said this wise' (A, B): D, 'said in this wyse'.

9, 'The cobbler' (A, D): B, 'Thys cobler'.

11, 'ye' (B, D): A, 'he'.

12, 'three pence' (A, B): D, 'saxtene pennies'.

Tale 9 (A.7, B.9, D.5)

1, 'in' (A, B): D, 'of'.

2, 'that' (B): D, 'and'.

4, 'as' (B, D): A, 'and'.

5, 'as' (A, B): absent in D.

5, 'specially' (A): B, 'especyall'; D, 'especiallie'.

8, 'say' (A, D): B, 'seyd'.

9, 'those' (A, B): D, 'thay'.

10, 'much' (A, B): D, 'far'.

Tale 10 (A.8, B.10, D.6)

1, 'which' (A, B): absent in D.

5, 'would' (A, B): D, 'suld'.

7, 'spoke to her' (A, B): D, 'spak'.

8, 'sake comfort' (A, D): B, 'sake to comfort'.

9, 'greatly' (B): absent in A and D.

11, 'Iwis' (A, B): D, 'Alace'.

15, 'yet' (A, B): absent in D.

16, 'sure … corpse' (A, D): B, 'sure alway of
  an other husband before that the corse'.

Tale 11 (A.9, B.11, D.7)

1-5, 'that kneeled … been for' (A, B): D, 'quhilk quhen sho was at the kirk burying hir husband, yair come a zong man vnto hir and rounded in hir eir, quhilk some thocht it had bene about'.

3-4, 'and spoke' (A): B, 'to speke'.

Tale 12 (A.10, B.12, D.8)

5, 'true' (A, D): B, 'trewth'.

9, 'perceive'(A, B): D, 'sie'.

9, 'gilt' (A, B): D, 'gold'.

9, 'but it is as' (A): B, 'but yt ys but as': D, 'but is as'.

Tale 13 (A.11, B.13)

1, 'which was' (A): absent in B.

18, 'man' (B): absent in A.

19, 'thy' (A): B, 'that'.

23, 'to' (B): absent in A.

35, 'He is' (B): A, 'and he is'.

44, 'than' (B): A, 'but'.

Tale 14 (A.12, B.14, D.10)

4, 'well' (A, B): absent in D.

9, 'then' (A, B): D, 'quhen'.

9, 'which' (A, B): D, 'hee'.

14, 'therefore' (A, B): D, 'thairof'.

15, 'the archdeacon' (D): A, 'the bysshoppe'; B, 'he'.

17, 'beforetime' (A, B): absent in D.

Tale 15 (A.13, B.15, D.11)

6, 'off the eel' (A, B): absent in D.

10, 'him' (A, D): B, 'the frere'.

13, 'ate' (emended): A 'ete'; B 'ete'; D, 'did eit'.

14, 'these' (A, B): D, 'those'.

Tale 16 (A.14, B.16)

4, 'whether' (B): A, 'and'.

17, 'fain' (A): absent in B.

41, 'may ye' (A): B, 'ye may'.

Tale 17 (A.15, B.17)

3, 'aught' (A): B, 'noght'.

13, 'to Him' (A): absent in B.

Tale 18 (A.16, B.18)

7, 'losing their' (B): A, 'lesynge of theyre'.

8, 'will' (B): A, 'mynde'.

30, 'him' (A): absent in B.

41, 'as he is' (A): B, 'ther for me'.

45, 'thought' (A): B, 'supposyng'.

47, 'fearing' (A): B, 'fered'.

47, 'somebody' (B): A, 'one'.

48, 'the' (A): absent in B.

64, 'into' (B): A, 'in'.

69, 'thereby' (B): A, 'by'.

84, 'had then' (B): A, 'there had'.

Tale 19 (A.17, B.19, D.12)

4, 'together' (A, B): absent in D.

14-5, 'ye shall ... have me' (A, B): absent in D.

15, 'for' (A, D): absent in B.

17, 'said' (B, D): A, 'saye'.

17, 'speak with' (A, D): B, 'seke'.

18, 'sure to' (A, D): B, 'sure euer to'.

21, 'stone' (A, B): absent in D.

Tale 20 (A.18, B.20)

4-5, 'a place of' (B): absent in A.

15, 'his mail' (B): A, 'hys maysters cloth sak'.

18, 'his mail' (B): A, 'the cloth sake'.

18, 'the potage' (A): B, 'that podege'.

20, 'mail' (B): A, 'cloth sake'.

21, 'other of' (A): B, 'other'.

28, 'mail' (B): A, 'cloth sake'.

31, 'that that is' (B): A, 'that is'.

32, 'bread' (B): absent in A.

35, 'the bread and the meat' (B): A, 'the broken mete'.

35, 'mail' (B): A, 'cloth sak'.

36, 'therefore put in your mail' (B): A, 'therin put'.

37, 'For' (B): absent in A.

Tale 21 (A.19, B.21, D.13)

3, 'heritage' (B, D): A, 'badheretage'.

5, 'come in' (B, D): A, 'to come in'.

7, 'had much trouble' (A, B): D, 'bein much troubled'.

7, 'have' (A, B): absent in D.

13, 'the' (A, D): B, 'a'.

13, 'Heaven' (A, B): D, 'his heritage'.

16, 'in trouble' (A, B): D, 'troublit'.

19, 'couldst' (B): A, 'coulde'; D, could'.

Tale 22 (A.20, B.22, D.14)

1-2, 'which had but one' (B): A, 'that had one'; D, 'that had a'.

7, 'him' (A, D): absent in B.

18, 'By God, yet I will' (A, B): D, 'By my trouth I will zit'.

21, 'so' (A, B): D, 'then'.

Tale 23 (A.21, B.23)

9, 'a' (B): absent in A.

Tale 24 (A.22, B.24)

2, 'off' (B): A, 'for'.

4, 'And he' (B): A, 'ⱺ'.

18-9, 'to rebuke their foolishness with' (B): A, 'for to rebuke them by'.

26, 'now' (A): absent in B.

Tale 25 (A.23, B.25)

1, 'himself' (B): A, 'hym'.

Tale 26 (A.24, B.26, D.15)

1, 'chandler' (A, B): D, 'Drapier'.

3, 'sore' (A, D): B, 'gretly'.

4, 'to her made' (A, B): D, 'maid to hir'.

11, 'o'clock' (A, B): D, 'houres'.

15, 'young' (B): absent in A and D.

17, 'Which' (A, B): D, 'quha'.

18, 'so did' (A, B): D, 'did so'.

20, 'more and louder' (A, B): D, 'moir lowder'.

20, 'it' (A, D): B, 'hym'.

25, 'By God's body' (A, B): D, 'surely'.

27, 'perceiving' (B, D): A, 'perceyued'.
28, 'for' (A, D): absent in B.
32, 'his head' (A, B): D, 'it'.
40, 'upon' (B): D, 'vp'.
49, 'horse' (A, B): D, 'horses'.
51, 'strewn' (A, D): B, 'strawyd'.
56, 'Morrow' (A, B): D, 'morning'.
58, 'shirt' (A '[sh]yrt', B): D, 'sark'.

59, 'had weened' (A, B): D, 'did think'.
64, 'segboard' (B): A, 'draught bord';
    D, 'draucht bord'.
66, 'he' (A): absent in B.
66, 'that' (A, B): absent in D.
69, 'nigh' (A, B): D, 'neir'.
71, 'well' (A, B): absent in D.
74, 'hatchets' (A, B): D, 'axes'.

Tale 27 (A.25, B.27, D.16)

5, 'anon' (A, B): D, 'thair'.
6, 'the' (A, B): D, 'hir'.

7, 'have' (A, D): B, 'on'.
9, 'me' (A, B): D, 'thee'.

Tale 28 (A.26, B.28, D.17)

1, 'company' (B): absent in D.
2, 'in' (B): D, 'and in'.
2, 'thus' (B): absent in D.
3, 'that' (A, D): absent in B.
3, 'pigs' (A, B): D, 'Gryses'.
6, 'pigs' (B): D, 'Gryses'.
9, 'gossips and showed her what' (B):
    D, 'Cummers quhair yat'.

10, 'taught' (A, B): D, 'tauld'.
10, 'pigs' (A, B): D, 'Gryses'.
11, 'answered her angrily' (B): A, 'answered
    angrely'; D, 'answered angerlie'.
12, 'drab' (A, B): D, 'ladron'.
14, 'woman' (A, D): B, 'wyfe'.
15, 'from' (B, D): A, 'fro'.

Tale 29 (A.27, B.29, D.18)

1, 'and a' (B, D): A, '&'.
4, 'Iwis' (A, B): D, 'Surely'.

9, 'your tooth' (A, B): D, 'it'.

Tale 30 (A.28, B.30)

3, 6, 12, 'absolve' (emended): A, B, 'assoyle'.
15, 'confessions' (B): A, 'conscyence'.

16, 'the' (B): absent in A.
16, 'it is a' (B): A, 'ye yt'.

Tale 31 (A.29, B.31)

8-9, 'take heed that he shot' (B): A, 'shote'.

24, 'the' (A): absent in B.

Tale 32 (A.30, B.32, D.19)

2, 'game' (B); A, 'gaue'.
6, 'somewhat grown' (A, D):
    B, 'growen some what'.
7, 'other' (A, D): absent in B.
8, 'commonly use' (A, B): D, 'vse commonly'.

8, 'and' (A, D): absent in B.
8, 'thus' (A, B): absent in D.
12, 'the t'one against the t'other' (A, B):
    D, 'the one against the vther'.
14, 'one' (A, B): D, 'a'.

Tale 33 (A.31, B.33, D.20)

2, 'niggard' (D): A, B 'nyggyn'.

10, 'which' (A, D): B, 'that'.

11, 'two' (B, D): A, 'iii' (also in title).

16, 'were' (B): D 'was'.

Tale 34 (A.32, B.34, D.21)

4, 'would' (A, D): absent in B.

8, 'This' (A, B): D, 'The'.

10, 'fortnight' (A, B): D, 'foure nichts'.

14, 'By God, friar' (A, B): D, 'By my faith'.

Tale 37 (A.36, B.37)

4, 5, 'bearer' (emended): A, B, 'beuer'.

14, 'an' (B): A, 'any'.

Tale 38 (A.37, B.38)

4, 'one' (B): absent in A.

8, 'so' (B): absent in A.

24, 'am' (A): B, 'wolbe'.

Tale 39 (A.38, B.39, D.22)

3, 'toothache' (A, B): D, 'worme'.

5, 'up' (A, B): D, 'in'.

6, 'therein for' (A, D): B, 'therfor'.

9, 'your' (A, D): B, 'thy'.

9-10, 'toothache' (A, B): D, 'worme'.

11, 'knees' (A, D): B, 'knee'.

32, 'an' (A, B): absent in D.

32, 'By God's Body' (A, B): D, 'A thou'.

39, 'incontinent' (A, B): D, 'and maid'.

40, 'to' (A, D): absent in B.

41-2, 'his toothache' (B): A, 'the tothake';
   D, 'the worme'.

43, 'the' (A): absent in B.

Tale 40 (A.39, B.40)

2, 'to' (B): A, 'in to'.

16, 'he' (A): B, 'she'.

20, 'would' (B): A, 'shold'.

34, 'Why' (A): absent in B.

47, 'it' (B): absent in A.

49, 'is' (A): B, 'were'.

Tale 41 (A.40, B.41)

4, 'at' (B): absent in A.

56, 'angrily' (B): A, 'angrey'.

59, 'which is in' (A): B, '.ys.'.

67, 'unto' (A): B, 'to'.

Tale 42 (A.41, B.42)

9, 'that' (B): absent in A.

10, 'with' (A): absent in B.

12, 'of' (B): absent in A.

20, 'the other' (B): A, 'him'.

24, 'broken' (B): A, 'broke'.

Tale 43 (A.33, B.43)

2, 'the' (A): B, 'a'.

16, 'that' (A): B, 'the'.

Tale 44 (A.42, B.44, D.23)

8, 'of us' (B): absent in D.

11-2, 'Then the other ... for' (A, B): absent in D.

13, 'and' (A, B): D, 'for'.

13, 'For' (A, B): D, 'becaus'.

15, 'thither' (A, B): absent in D.

14, 'and' (A, D): absent in B.

14, 'saith he ... in Hell' (A, B): D, 'sayeth that he sal go to hel'.

Tale 45 (A.43, B.45, D.25)

2, 'never come' (A, B): D, 'come neuer'.

6, 'see one play' (A, B): D, 'saw ane lute'.

8, 'at wedding' (A, B): D, 'sene'.

12, 'sweetliest' (B): D, 'sweetest'.

Tale 46 (A.44, B.46, D.25)

2, 'gotten' (B): absent in D.

3, 'charged her to tell' (B, D): A, 'that ... [t]ell'.

7, 'thereof' (A, B): D, 'of the chylde'.

8-9, 'I not' (B, D): A, 'not [I]'.

Tale 47 (A.45, B.47, D.26)

2, 'and' (A as read by Singer - the surviving fragment may read '[Tem]ys &' but none of the letters survives intact): absent in B and D.

3, 'the most quickest fellow' (A, B): D, 'ane of the quickest in the warlde'.

3-4, 'rode alway' (A, B): D, 'euer ryding'.

5, 'quod he' (B): absent in D.

5, 'thou' (A, D): absent in B.

6, 'for' (D): absent in B.

7, 'withal' (D): B, 'with'.

9, 'thou' (A, D): absent in B.

12, 'Why!' (B): absent in A and D.

13, 'By my ... cannot tell' (A with partial lacuna, B): D, 'Neyther can I do sa, saide he'.

13, 'tell' (B): absent in A (for D, see above).

21, 'many a man' (A, D): B, 'manny men'.

21, 'lieth' (A): B, 'lye'; D, 'lyes'.

23, 'thou' (A): absent in B; D, 'ye'.

25, 'the' (B): D, 'that'.

30, 'do it' (B): A, 'doist'; D, 'doest it'.

32, 'although ... peradventure' (A, B): absent in D.

32, 'had' (B): absent in A.

32, 'peradventure' (A): absent in B.

Tale 48 (A.46, B.48)

5, 'in all haste, he' (emended): B, 'in all the haste'.

17, 'property' (B): A, '[proper]tyes'.

Tale 49 (A.47, B.49, D.29)

3, 'therefore' (A, B): D, 'for it'.

5, 'upon condition' (B): D, 'vpon that condition'.

6-7, 'forty shillings' (A, B): D, 'twenty poundis'.

7, 'whereto' (B): A, 'wher[to]'; D, 'quhairof'.

9, 'such' (A, B): D, 'the'.

10, 'nigh' (A, B): D, 'neir'.

11, 'deliver' (A '[deliu]er', D): B, 'gyue'.

11, 'this man' (A): B, 'hym'; D, 'to this man'.

12, 'a pin's point' (A, B): D, 'a pynne, a point'.

15, 'forty shillings' (A, B): D, 'xxl'.

16-7, 'being aggrieved' (A, B): D, 'seing him greued'.

20, 'a-town' (A, B): D, 'off Town'.

20, 'this matter' (A): B, 'this'; D, 'the mater'.

28, 'forty shillings' (B): D, 'xx punds'.

30, 'into' (B): A, D 'in'.

32, 'it' (A, D): absent in B.

33, 'forty shillings' (A, B): D, 'twentie poundes'.

34, 'through it' (A, D): B, 'vp thrugh'.

Tale 50 (A.48, B.50)

18-9, 'for thee is' (A): B, 'is for the'.

39, 'tale' (A): absent in B.

Tale 51 (A.49, B.51, D.30)

1, 'that' (B): D, 'quhilk'.
5, 'How' (B): absent in D.
6, 'thy' (B): D, 'the'.

8, 'Sir' (A, B): D, 'sirra'.
12, 'saith' (A, B): D, 'sayis'.

Tale 53 (A.51, B.53, D.31)

2, 'back' (A, B): D, 'black'.
3, 'jesting' (A, B): D, 'moking'.
5, 'the courtier espied in him' (A, B): D, 'he saw'.

9, 'wise' (A, B): D, 'way'.
9, 'I lightly' (B): A, 'lyghtlye'; D, 'commonly I'.
11, 'useth' (A): B, 'vsed'.

Tale 54 (A.52, B.54)

17, 'give' (B): A, 'haue'.

33, 'thee' (A): B, 'ye' (the usual ligature for 'the').

Tale 55 (A.53, B.55)

22, 'wherefore' (A): B, 'Where'.

25, 'this' (A): B, 'his'.

Tale 56 (A.54, B.56)

2, 'and though' (B): A, 'all though'.
4, 'the Twelve Articles' (B): A, 'xii. artycles'.
14, 'fetched' (emended): A, B, 'fet'.

20, 'the Holy Church' (A): B, 'holy chyrche'.
26, 'and' (B): absent in A.

Tale 57 (A.55, B.57)

4, 'was' (B): absent in A.
8, 'other' (B): absent in A.

13, 'and to help' (A): B, '⁊ helpe'.
26, 'unleefully' (B): A, 'vnlaufully'.

Tale 58 (A.56, B.58, D.27)

1, 'thus' (A, B): D, 'on this'.

1, 'wise' (A, D): B, 'wyfe'.

Tale 60 (A.58, B.60, D.32)

2, 'laudable and' (A, B): absent in D.
4, 'sermons' (A, D): B, 'sermon'.
7, 'gossip' (A, B): D, 'cummer'.

14, 'so openly . . . her beheld' (A, B): absent in D.
16, 'more' (A, B): D, 'most'.
17, 'did laugh' (A, B): D, 'merely lauched'.

Tale 61 (A.59, B.61)

11, 'prisoner' (B): A, 'prysoners'.

22, 'greater' (B): A, 'great'.

Tale 62 (A.60, B.62, D.33)

1, 'had' (A, D): B, 'hath'.

4, 'full oft' (B): absent in A and D.

9, 'born' (A, B): absent in D.

10, 'therefore, that is thus' (A in parenthesis, B):
   D, 'thairfoir, and that is this'

16, 'Wherefore' (A, B): D, 'quhairof'.

18, 'upon' (B): A, D 'on'.

19, 'desirous' (A, B): D, 'being desirous'.

20, 'demanded' (B): A, 'he demaunded';
   D, '[h]ee demanded'.

31, 'taught' (A, D): D, 'tauld'.

33, 'taught' (B): D, 'tald'.

34, 'to' (B): absent in D.

36, 'now she' (B): D, 'scho now'.

42, 'but I' (A, B): D, 'and'.

43, 'yet' (A, B): absent in D.

44, 'but yet . . . to speak' (A, B): absent in D.

44, 'yet' (B): A, 'and'.

Tale 63 (A.61, B.63, D.34)

5, 'Among' (A, B): D, 'Among all'.

Tale 64 (A.62, B,64)

13, 'and' (A): absent in B.

18, 'that' (B): absent in A.

27, 'her' (A): B, 'the'.

27, 'and' (A): absent in B.

17, 'again' (B): absent in A and D.

19, 'it' (A, D): absent in B.

20, 'roost' (A, B): D, 'roof'.

21, 'up' (A, B): D, 'vpon'.

23, 'so' (A, B): D, 'hee'.

Tale 65 (A.63, B.65, D.35)

1, 'and fortunate' (B): absent in D.

2-3, 'great puissance and army' (B):
   D, 'a greit puisant Armie'.

4, 'both the' (B): D, 'the two'.

6, 'on' (A, B): D, 'upon'.

6, 'of' (A, B): absent in D.

7, 'the noise' (A, B): D, 'heiring the noyse'.

7, 'the courage' (A, B): D, 'his corage'.

8, 'him retain' (A, B): D, 'retayne him'.

9, 'squire' (A, B): absent in D.

16, 'that' (B): absent in A and D.

16, 'was' (A, B): D, 'played'.

17, 'the' (A, B): D, 'a'.

25, 'for' (A, D): absent in B.

26, 'therefore' (A): absent in B and D.

Tale 66 (A.64, B.66, D.36)

3, 'came' (A, B): D, 'He come'.

10, 'bade' (A): B, 'had'; D, 'bad hir'.

10, 'after, he' (A, B): absent in D.

11, 'thereto' (B): absent in A and D.

13, 'so' (A, B): absent in D.

Tale 67 (A.65, B.67)

10, 'in the' (A): absent in B.

16, 'a twelvemonth' (A): B, 'at twelfe month'.

334

Tale 68 (A.66, B.68)

7, 'the' (A); absent in B.

Tale 69 (A.67, B.69, D.37)

4-5, 'a vacation time' (emended):
  A, B, 'a vocacyon tyme'; D, 'the vacants'.
6, 'on' (A, D): B, 'in'.
11, 'to school' (B): D, 'at scole'.

12, 'thou' (D): absent in B.
12, 'hast learned' (B): D, 'learnest'.
20, 'here' (A, B): D, 'thair'.
25, 'for' (A, B): absent in D.

Tale 70 (A.68, B.69)

22, 'out' (A): absent in B.

Tale 71 (A.69, B.71)

2, 'a' (A): absent in B.
21, 'Coll my dog' (B): A, 'all my dogges'.

23, 'say' (B): A, 'sayd'.

Tale 72 (A.70, B.72, D.9)

1, 'so' (A, B): absent in D.
4-5, 'after, he … asleep, came' (A, B):
  D, 'being a sleip, the man and wife come efter'
6, 'And' (A, B): absent in D.

7, 'the market' (A, B): D, 'market'.
12, 'shall' (A, B): D, 'will'.
12, 'waketh' (A, B): D, 'riseth'.
12-3, 'whom … wife' (A, B): absent in D.

Tale 73 (A.71, B.73)

4, 'Shottery' (B); A, 'shorte space'.

Tale 74 (A.72, B.74, D.38)

3-4, 'words angry … other, and' (B):
  D, 'angry wordes, and being displeased
  one with an other'.

5, 'and' (D): absent in B.
8, 'was so' (A, B): absent in D.

Tale 75 (A.73, B.75, D.39)

1, 'preacher' (A, B): D, 'Freir'.
1, 'the' (B, D): absent in A.
1-2, 'which preached … God and' (A, B):
  D, 'being preching verie fond things'.

4, 'space' (A, B): D, 'compas'.
9, 'then' (A, D): B, 'tell then'.

Tale 76 (A.74, B.76)

6-8, 'against his … life, except' (emended following Singer): A, 'agaynst his lyfe except coming he wolde be redy harneysed & wolde put him in ieopardye of his comynge'; B, 'agaynst his lyf execept coming he wolde be redy harnesyd & wolde put hym in ieoperdy of his comyng'.

11, 'into' (B): A, 'in at'.
11, 'set' (B): A, 'and set'.

26, 'she' (B): absent in A.

Tale 77 (A.75, B.77, D.40)

3, 'were' (B): D, 'was'.

Tale 79 (A.77, B.79)

7, 'that' (A): absent in B.

Tale 80 (A.78, B.80)

9, 'and perceiving' (B): A, 'perceiuyng'.
14, 'and' (A): absent in B.

17, 'holy' (A): B, 'holyly'.

Tale 81, (A.79, B.81)

9, 'prayer' (A): B, 'pray'.

Tale 82, (A.80, B.82, D.41)

4, 'killed' (B): D, 'had killed'.
9, 'full' (A, B): D, 'so'.

13, 'other' (emended): B, 'grer'.
15, 'as fast as' (A, D): B, 'as fast'.

Tale 83 (A.81, B.83)

2, 'well' (A): absent in B.

21, 'upon Good Friday' (A): B, 'as on yester day'.

Tale 84 (A.82, B.84, D.42)

1, 'the' (A, B): absent in D.
9, 'all' (B): absent in A and D.
10, 'By God, sir' (B): D, 'No, no'.

14, 'again' (B): absent in A and D.
19, 'that' (A, B): D, 'the'.
24, 'ye' (A, D): B, 'it'.

Tale 86 (A.84, B.86, C.1, D.43)

4, 'by God' (A, B): absent in D.

10, 'in' (B): absent in C and D.

Tale 87 (A.85, B.87, C.2)

1, 'On' (A, C): B, 'IN'.
2, 'got' (A, B): C, 'gotten'.
6, 'the priest' (B): A, C, 'he'.
7, 'in' (A, B): absent in C.

13, 'in the roof' (B, C): A, 'in rofe'.
17, 'said in sport' (A, C): absent in B.
19, 'shortly' (B): absent in A and C.
21, 'By this' (A, B): C, 'By this tale'.

Tale 88 (A.86, B.88, C.3)

3, 'afore' (A, B): C, 'before'.
3, 'sitten' (A, B): C, 'had sytten'.
3, 'and came' (A, B): C, 'came'.

8, 'up' (B): absent in A and C.
10, 'Wherewith' (A, B): C, 'Ɵ herwith'.
11, 'awaked' (A): B, 'wakyd'.

Tale 90 (A.88, B.90, C.4, D.44)

4, 'Prepare mihi modicum' (A, B):
  D, 'prepare mihi nisi modicum'.
9, 'ate' (emended): A, B, 'ete'; C, 'eate'; D, 'did eate'.

10, 'displeased' (A, B, D): C, 'displeaseth'.
11-2, 'in making great dinners' (A, C): absent in B.

Tale 92 (A.89, B.92, C.5)

4, 'into' (B): A, C, 'to'.

Tale 93 (A.90, B.93, C.6)

1, 'the' (B): absent in A and C.
8, 'ye' (B, C): A, 'he'.

9, 'therewith being' (A, B): C, 'beynge ther with'.
11, 'heads' (B, C): A, 'hede'.

Tale 94 (A.91, B.94, C.7)

6, 'other' (B): absent in A and C.
13, 'on the groat and nothing' (A '... grote &
  [no]thing', B): absent in C.
17, 'marvellest' (B 'merueloust'): C, 'meruaylous'.

19, 'Jesus' (C): B, 'Jesu'.
23, 'By this' (A, B): C, 'By this tale'.
24, 'be foolish' (A, B): C, 'be so foolyshe'.

Tale 95 (A.92, B.95, C.8)

9, 'thus' (A, B): absent in C.

Tale 96 (A.93, B.96, C.9)

4, 'his' (A, C): absent in B.
11, 'elder' (B): A, 'eldest'.

14, 'dost' (B): A, 'dost thou'.

Tale 97 (A.94, B.97)

2, 'fair' (A): B, 'the fair'.

Tale 98 (B.98)

18, 'niggardship' (emended): B, 'nygynshyp'.

Tale 99 (A.95, B.99, C.10, D.45)

1, 'northern man' (B): D, 'Sowtherneman'.
3, 'lord then had war' (A 'lorde than hadde ...', B):
  D, 'was at feid'.
4, 'northern man' (A, B): D, 'southernman'.
5, 'Good's Banes' (adapted): A, '... ddes byens';
  B, 'goodys byens'; D, 'coks bons'.
5, 'northern man' (A, B): D, 'southern'.
6, 'is' (B): D, 'am'.
8, 'that' (B): absent in D.

11-2, 'northern man' (B): D, Southerneman'.
12, 'thou' (B, D): C, 'ye'.
15, 'God's Sowl' (adapted): A, B, C, 'goddes sale';
  D, 'cocks saull'.
15, 'is' (A 'as', B, C): D, 'am'.
15, 'all' (C, D): absent in B.
16, 'head' (B): absent in C and D.
17, 'in' (B, C): D, 'to'.

Tale 100 (A.96, B.100)

15, 'good' (A): absent in B.

41, 'commandment' (B): A, '[comm]and'.

Tale 101 (A.97, C.11, D.46)

4, 'manners' (C, D): A, 'maner'.

8, 'known' (A 'kn[owen], D): C, 'a knowen'.

14, 'said' (D): absent in C.

15, 'of it' (A): absent in C and D.

17, 'courtier' (A, C): D, 'the courtier'.

17, 'that' (A): absent in C and D.

19, 'perceived' (A, C): D, 'perceyuing'.

20-1, 'thou wast' (A): C, 'ye waste'; D, 'you was'.

Tale 102 (A.99, C.12, D.47)

8, 'surely' (C, D): A, 'sure'.

14, 'kerchiefs' (A): D, 'a curchie'.

Tale 103 (A.100, D.1)

2, 'that' (A): absent in D.

3, 'oversea' (A): D 'ouer the Sea'.

5, 'that' (D): absent in A.

9, 'wooed' (A): D, 'suited'.

10, 'content' (A): D, 'content that'.

10, 'which' (A): D, 'quha'.

14, 'Then' (A): D, 'But'.

18, 'busy' (A): D, 'beside'.

Bibliography

Ames, Joseph, 1749, *Typographical Antiquities: Being an historical account of printing in England*, J. Robinson, London.

Arber, Edward (ed.) 1875–94, *A Transcript of the Registers of the Company of Stationers of London 1554–1640 A.D.* 5 Volumes, London.

Axton, Richard (ed.) 1979, *Three Rastell Plays: Four Elements, Calisto and Melebea, Gentleness and Nobility*, D. S.Brewer Ltd, Cambridge.

Betteridge, Thomas & Walker, Greg, 2012, *The Oxford Handbook of Tudor Drama*, OUP, Oxford.

Blayney, Peter W. M. 2013, *The Stationers' Company and the Printers of London 1501-1557*, CUP, Cambridge.

Boorde, Andrew, 1540 (reprinted 1565), *Merie Tales of the Made Men of Gotam*, London.

Boorde, Andrew, 1565-6 (reprinted 1626), *Geystes of Skoggan*, London.

Boorde, Andrew, 1542 (ed. F. J. Furnivall, 1870), *Fyrst Boke of the Introduction of Knowledge*, London.

Bowen, Barabara C. (ed.) 1988, *One Hundred Renaissance Jokes: An Anthology*, Summa, Birmingham Alabama.

Bracciolini, Poggio, 1470 (1879), *The Facetiae or Jocose Tales of Poggio*, Isidore Liseux, Paris.

Brewer, Derek (ed.) 1973, 1996, *Medieval Comic Tales*, D. S. Brewer (Boydell & Brewer), Cambridge.

Charteris, Robert (printer) 1603, *The Thrie Tales of the Thrie Priests of Peblis*, Edinburgh; facsimile edition 1969 by Da Capo Press, New York.

Deutermann, Allison K., & Kiséry, András (edd.) 2013, *Formal Matters: Reading the Materials of English Renaissance Literature*, Manchester.

Devereux, Edward James, 1999, *A Bibliography of John Rastell*, McGill-Queen's University Press, Montreal.

Furness, H. H. (ed.) 1871-1913 (1963), *Much Adoe About Nothing, A New Variorum Edition of Shakespeare*, Vol.12, New York.

Gairdner, James, 1876, *The Historical Collections of a Citizen of London*, London.

Greene, Robert, 1591 (1923), *A notable Discovery of Coosnage*, London.

Halliwell, James Orchard (ed.) 1840, *The Merry Tales of the Wise Men of Gotham*, London.

Hazlitt, William Carew (ed.) 1864, *Shakespeare Jest Books: Reprints of the very rare jest-books supposed to have been used by Shakespeare*, Willis & Sotheran, London.

Hazlitt, William Carew (ed.) 1887, *A Hundred Merry Tales: The earliest English jest-book*, J. W. Jarvis & Son, London.

Heywood, John, 1562, *Three Hundred Epigrams upon Three Hundred Proverbs*, London.

King, Pamela, & Davidson, Clifford, 2000, *The Coventry Corpus Christi Plays*, Michigan.

Klaf, Franklin S. & Hurwood, Bernhardt J. (edd.) 1964, *A Hundred Merry Tales*, The Citadel Press, New York.

Langham, Robert, 1580 (ed. R. J. P. Kuin, 1983) *A Letter*, E. J. Brill, Leiden.

Latimer, Hugh, 1549 (2010), *The seconde [seventh] Sermon of Maister Hughe Latimer*, London.

Munro, Ian, 2004, 'Shakespeare's Jestbook: Wit, Print, Performance' 89-113 in *ELH* 71.1

Munro, Ian, 2007, '*A womans answer is neuer to seke*': Early Modern Jestbooks, 1526–1635: Essential Works for the Study of Early Modern Women: Series III, Part 2, Vol.8, Routledge, London.

Oesterley, Dr Herman (ed.) 1866, *Shakespeare's Jest Book: A Hundred Mery Talys from the only perfect copy known*, John Russell Smith, London.

Rawlinson, Kent, 2012, 'Hall's Chronicle and the Greenwich Triumphs of 1527' 402-28 in Betteridge & Walker 2012

Ray, John, 1670, *A Collection of English Proverbs*. Cambridge.

Reed, A. W. 1926, *Early Tudor Drama*, Methuen, London.

Roberts, R. J. 1979 'John Rastell's Inventory of 1538', 34-42 in *The Library*, 6th series, I.

Routledge, George (ed.) 1845, *Shakespeare's Merry Tales*, Routledge, Warne & Routledge, London.

Scot, Reginald, 1584 (ed. B. Nicholson, 1886), *The Discoverie of Witchcraft*, London.

Sharp, Thomas, 1825, *A Dissertation on the Pageants or dramatic Mysteries anciently performed at Coventry*, Coventry.

Singer, Samuel Weller (ed.) 1815, *Shakespeare's Jest Book: Part II*, C Whittingham, Chiswick.

Skelton, John, 1567, *Merie tales newly imprinted made by Master Skelton Poet Laureat*, Thomas Colwell, London.

Smyth, Adam, 2013, "Divines into dry Vines': forms of jesting in Renaissance England' in Deutermann & Kiséry, 2013

Somerset, J. A. B. (ed.) 1974, 2013, *Four Tudor Interludes*, Bloomsbury, London.

Tarlton, Richard (attrib.) 1590 (ed. J. O. Halliwell, 1844), *Tarltons Newes out of Purgatorie*, London.

Thomas, Keith, 1977, 'The place of laughter in Tudor and Stuart England', 77-81 in *Times Literary Supplement*, 21 Jan. 1977, London.

Thompson, Craig R. (ed.) 1997, *Collected Works of Erasmus: Colloquies*, University of Toronto Press, Toronto.

Tilley, Morris Palmer, 1950, *A dictionary of the proverbs in England in the sixteenth and seventeenth centuries*, University of Michigan Press, Ann Arbor.

Unger, F. W. 1864, 'Zur Shakespeare Litteratur', 142-4 in *Serapeum Nr.9*

Wakelin, Daniel, 2012, 'Gentleness and Nobility, John Rastell, c.1525-27', 192-206 in Betteridge & Walker 2012

Zall, P. M. (ed.) 1963, *A Hundred Merry Tales, and other jestbooks of the fifteenth and sixteenth centuries*, University of Nebraska Press (Bison Books 171), Lincoln, Nebraska.

Lightning Source UK Ltd.
Milton Keynes UK
UKHW012220271220
375841UK00005B/651